# STAINED

## GLASS

## STEP BY STEP

Patricia Ann Daley

D1581613

David & Charles

A DAVID & CHARLES BOOK

First published in the UK in 2003

First published in the USA in 2003 by North Light Books,
Cincinnati, Ohio

A catalogue record for this book is available from the British
Library.

ISBN 0 7153 1712 1 paperback

Printed in China by Regent Publishing Services
for David & Charles
Brunel House    Newton Abbot    Devon

Visit our website at www.davidandcharles.co.uk

David & Charles books are available from all good bookshops;
alternatively you can contact our Orderline on (0)1626 334555 or
write to us at FREEPOST EX2 110, David & Charles Direct, Newton
Abbot, TQ12 4ZZ (no stamp required UK mainland).

# TaBLe of contents

# acknowledgments

I wish to thank Glass Crafters for allowing me to photograph the new, updated grinders and saws available to the hobbyist, and Richard Setti for use of his thought-provoking chess game, "Futility of War". Thanks to Calvin Sloan at Star Bevel for an interesting afternoon exploring his finished work on display and in storage.

Special thanks to my customers for commissioned work and for their patience in waiting for completed jobs being photographed, either as work in progress or finished pieces...and to my students for their works.

My deepest appreciation goes to Harold and Shirley Wyman for their help in creating stained glass pieces and taking all the photographs for this book...and for that special trip to Maggie Valley, N.C.

I'm grateful to Seymour Isenberg for his personal support and encouragement during the past two years.

And of course, thank you, Don and Janet Traynor for requesting this book, and to Steve Bridges and Laura Couallier for using their combined design vision and abilities in presenting this finished work.

# aBOUT THE auTHOr

The path that eventually led Pat Daley to distinguished achievements as a glass artist, author and teacher, as with many of us is replete with unanticipated experiences that in part, guide us to our career niche. A Massachusetts native, her family moved frequently before a defining time in Maine. It began as a family experience. Pat, a high school junior and her parents studied and began the practice of "silversmith," spending most summer weekends presenting at craft shows. A Westbrook College (Maine) graduate, Pat worked in printing, hospitality and radio broadcasting while harboring a growing, serious attraction to glass crafting, especially stained glass.

Then in 1976, Pat and John Daley opened a home-studio to work in glass in Scarborough, Maine. Success led to establishing their retail/teaching studio, J & P Stained Glass in Portland in 1989, and soon board of director seats on the prestigious League of Maine Craftsmen.

For the past 7 years Pat has operated Kaleidoscope Stained Glass, in Sarasota, FL for teaching everything stained glass, and producing custom commission work for contract and residential clients. A contributor to books by other glass artists, Pat previously wrote "Patterns by Pat — 8 Stepping Stones," and is currently working on a sequel.

# INTRODUCTION

The popularity of stained glass experienced resurgence in the late 1960's due to the efforts of the crafts movement. For a long time it was strictly the realm of the glass man, working in a commission studio crafting windows primarily for churches, public buildings and some residential work. If you wanted to work in stained glass, it required searching for a studio that would take-in an individual to learn by observing. A local glass supply shop, as such, didn't exist, and when it was determined that working in glass was a viable business for the general hobbyists, the large studios began to realize that their hold on the craft was weakening. However, the studios needed to realize the future and popularity of the stained glass trade would be enhanced and not diminished as hobbyists, collectors and the next generation of craftsmen arrived. Due to the limited information available to the public about crafting stained glass, Seymour and Anita Isenberg wrote "How to Work in Stained Glass" widely considered the bible of the craft. Today, the renaissance in stained glass continues its far-reaching popularity with glass being used more in homes, commercial applications and even on the sets of your favorite TV shows.

The purpose of this book is to give you a basic working knowledge of the stained glass craft. A description of how glass is made and the different types of glass begins your introduction to the wide variety of glass available. The following chapters explain how to set up a work area and the tools you will use. Detailed instructions with accompanying photographs will show you how to safely cut glass into shapes. A discussion on designing will guide you to create patterns for construction with the *lead came* or the *copper foil* process. Instruction on soldering and reinforcing for both techniques will assist you in building a lasting object d'art in stained glass. An illustrated step-by-step guide will explain how a lead came window is made, and how a copper foil panel is built and framed. This book offers five stained glass projects, with patterns included, if you wish to "build along" and begin to experience more fully, the art of stained glass.

While expressions in stained glass are widely seen and can reach fine art status, the scope of this book barely touches on complex techniques such as glass being painted and shaped in a kiln; and does not include precise surface treatments such as engraving or sandblasting.

Items such as jewelry boxes, mirrors, clocks, planters, wall sconces, and lately, mosaics can all be crafted with glass. This book, then, is a primer on the proper techniques to begin a satisfying hobby.

Pat Daley

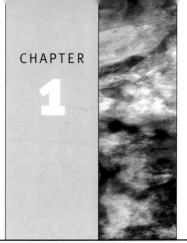

# THE BASICS OF GLASS

Glass is a mystical substance that serves many purposes. A solid liquid, it protects you from the elements as a window, while allowing you to see the very dynamic it shields you against. It's myriad colors inspire awe in the soul and have invoked the senses throughout the ages from simple, pleasing designs to overwhelming pictorial vistas, to taking an abstract form representing the personal expression of the artist. Glass is seen in our daily lives in so many forms that we often take it for granted—a juice bottle to a computer monitor picture tube—yet if everything glass were suddenly removed from our lives, the impact would be monumental.

Glass is made from elements of the earth—silica sand with about one percent iron, soda ash, limestone and borax. In the Middle Ages, when cathedral building was the highest form of architecture, glass was "stained" by adding metallic oxides to an already molten batch of basic glass to color it. Today, for machine made glass, the metal oxides are carefully measured along with the rest of "the recipe," dry

**Bird of Prey**
Seymour Isenberg

Painted antique and leaded glass from the artist's personal collection.

mixed, then poured into large crucibles and placed in the furnaces to be melted. Some of the metal oxides used are dichrome, which yields green; copper will turn the clear batch to shades of blue, but add cobalt for the deep rich hues. Reds, oranges, shades of yellow come from cadmium or in many of the deeper jewel like colors like gold salts. This is why "gold-pinks" and "reds" will always have a much higher price regardless of the manufacturer. The formulas for mixing color into glass are exact with the proper humidity and temperature playing an important part.

Once the crucible is heated to the proper temperature and the contents are a white-hot color, a ladle is used to scoop liquid glass, carrying it to the mixing slab and milling rollers. On the mixing slab, any single or combination of colors are twirled with a two-pronged fork. The glass is now beginning to cool to shades of orange and needs to be quickly placed in the fountain, on top of the rollers, to be milled to an even thickness. This is the stage where textures are added to the glass. The bottom roller has the engraved pattern—hammered, "thin spaghetti" or reed-like lines which emboss the surface of the glass. Ripple and granite textures are made by loosely fitting the hammered roller and

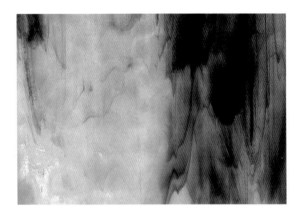

Youghiogheny:
Pink and ice
white glass

allowing it to slip on the glass as it passes by. The thickness of the glass is now at 1/8", becoming a dull orange/red and flowing onto a moving conveyor belt into the *annealing lehr*. This is a type of oven that controls the rate of the glass cooling by evenly heating the glass, and transporting it from a hot section to a cooler one in order to properly temper the glass. When it reaches the end of the lehr, it is cold and the colors now show. It is cut into lengths varying from 42" to 48" and the width is trimmed to 24" to 32" depending on the manufacturer, then packed in crates and shipped to the distributors. This is a very basic description of how *machined glass* is made. Several large companies seemingly have endless conveyors of glass running 24 hours a day. In addition, there are companies that produce a more unique or specialty glass in short runs resulting in a distinctive craft palate for the marketplace. Accordingly, each glass color is identified by a number or number/letter combination assigned by the manufacturer for color, density and texture, and matched against a master sample for production consistency.

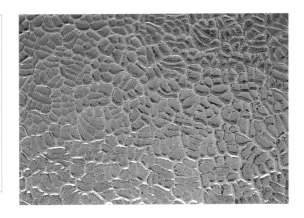

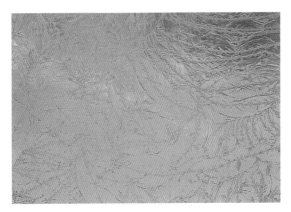

## Antique Glass

True *antique glass* is made in a wholly different fashion. This glass is mixed, melted in a furnace as the *glass blower* steps in to gather liquid glass on the end of a *pontil rod*, and blows it into a cylinder shape, like a bottle with a bottom and neck. The neck and bottom are cut off leaving the open-ended cylinder. Next, it is cut down the sides to make two halves and placed in an oven to heat where the raised sides relax and lay down to form two sheets of stained glass. The beauty of antique glass is the uneven thickness, hence the subtle variations from light to dark color within the sheet, and the "seeds" or larger "ox-eyes" from trapped air bubbles within the glass. Antique glass is sometimes tricky to cut, as it may not lie flat on the table and the thickness resists breaking, but the results with antique jewel tones are breathtaking. Hand blown glass is made mostly in England, France and Germany and cost a little more due to the importing but is worth it. There is new machine assisted antique glass from France and Germany, which is consistent in thickness and colors, but is seedless compared to the variations found in the mouth-blown glass.

**English Rose**
Harold & Shirley Wyman,
Bradenton, FL

Textured cathedral glass and
English Muffle used in master
bath to mask a window.

## Cathedral Glass

*Cathedral glass* can described as "colored window pane glass", 1/8" thick, can have an embossed texture, and is available in a wide color range. Glass on the market with trade names such as Spectrum's "Waterglass", new "Rough Rolled" and "Artique" are cathedral type glass with light surface texturing to give a highlight effect. *Granite* and *ripple textures* in cathedral glass are quite striking in sunlight as they sparkle. Another texture called "glue chip" is created when cathedral glass has been lightly sandblasted and applied animal hide glue dries on the surface. This strong glue then will pull the surface of the glass and actually peel-off flakes of glass. The result is a feathery or frost appearance on the glass.

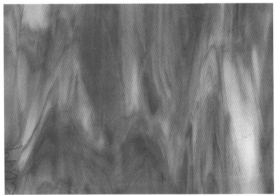

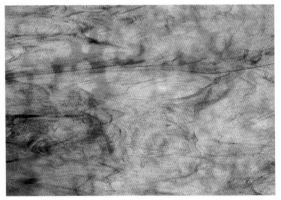

**Rose Bouquet**
Harold & Shirley Wyman,
Bradenton, FL

Oval panel with clear glue chip and English Muffle glass. From a drawing in "162 Traditional Stained Glass Designs" by Dover Books

**from top to bottom**

Bullseye Glass: Blue opal plum streaky cathedral glass

Spectrum Glass: Blue/white opalescent glass

Gecko Glass: Green/white/ ruby red glass

Spectrum Glass: Red/white wispy glass

**from top
to bottom**

Youghiogheny:
Reflected lighted
glass

Youghiogheny:
transmitted
lighted glass

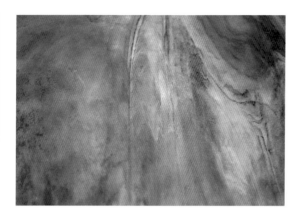

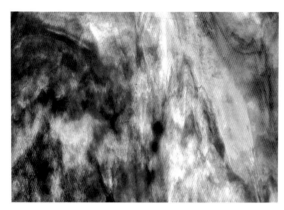

## Opalescent Glass

*Opalescent glass* is unique as it can exhibit shape and
shadow, as well as color. This glass can be 2 to 3, even
up to 5 colors mixed in a sheet to achieve swirling
color on a background. This technique is what I call
the "painted brushstroke of stained glass." You can
pick the right curl of purple with a highlight of white
to make a petal of an iris with depth and a spot of sunlight on it. This glass has color running in one direction
(usually top to bottom of a sheet that was fed into the
milling rollers) and the effect can be referred to as the
"grain." *Physically, glass has no grain as compared to
wood* so there is no need to be concerned about cutting across the sheet from any direction.

This glass can be subdivided into:

a) *wispy*—more clear or cathedral color than solid/
   opaque color = very transparent,

b) *translucent*—more opaque color than clear/
   cathedral color = somewhat transparent, and

c) *opaque* – dense, mixed color = cannot see
   through it.

These glasses can also be textured and, again, this will
diffuse the light through the piece. Opalescent glass
will require careful consideration when choosing colors. This is the only glass that will be seen in reflected
light as well as transmits light through it.

At night, antique and cathedral window glass disap-
pears into darkness while opalescent glass takes on
another appearance with front illumination from interi-
or room light. A stained glass window at night or a
lampshade during the day will appear as the glass
does when unlit—somewhat muted. A window in day-
light and an illuminated lampshade in the evening will
have brighter, vibrant colors. When choosing glass for
your projects, it is important to consider how it will
appear with and without light to gain the best results.

There are a wide variety of manufacturers who produce
a multitude of textured and pattern glass from bamboo
to sycamore leaves to names such as "stream X" with
some of these patterns having existed for almost a
hundred years or merely the last few years. All of these
should be cut on the smoother or back side, so when
laying out your pattern piece on them—don't forget to
reverse the pattern and cut *face side* down.

## Dichroic Glass

Another modern glass is *dichroic*. This glass changes color depending on the angle viewed and features combinations of magenta-blue, yellow-red with a variety of textures on clear glass or black. A thin metallic coating gives this effect the appearance of silver in reflected light. This glass is the most costly to purchase due to the process used to produce it.

ABOVE
**top row,
left to right**

Dichroic on black glass

Textures: Ripple, Fibroid, Standard, Radium

**bottom row,
left to right**

Dichroic on clear glass

Textures: Fipple, Fibroid, Smooth

ABOVE
**Fused Jewelry**
Pat Daley,
Kaleidoscope Stained Glass,
Sarasota, FL

Oval pendant with dichroic chips in a gold wire wrap framework. Teardrop earrings with wave pattern dichroic glass in gold wire wrap framework.

LEFT
**Dichroic Rose**
Pat Daley,
Kaleidoscope Stained Glass,
Sarasota, FL

The colors of the rose change with point-of-view.

**Dalle perfume bottle**
Pat Daley,
Kaleidoscope Stained
Glass, Sarasota, FL
Faceted dalle glass with
nuggets, copper foiled
and soldered together
to hold a glass vial.

BELOW
**Sunburst**
Calvin Sloan,
Star Bevel Studio,
Riverview, FL
Dalle de Verre glass
cast in black matrix
for brilliant color.

## Dalle de Verre

Dalle de Verre or *slab glass* is a form of stained glass—
the mixing process is the same but the molten glass is
poured into wooden molds to create a brick 8" x 11"
and 1" thick. This cannot be scored and broken in the
traditional manner, but it can be used in block form or
chipped and faceted to be mounted in special epoxy
cement. In addition, smaller pieces can be used with
copper foil for unique effects. These pieces have the
effect of precious jewels when seen in sunlight.

Wissmach Glass:
Iridescent
patterned glass

## Iridescent Glass

Another added type of coating to enhance glass is a
wash applied over the glass to give a rainbow effect.
This is call iridescent or iridized glass. It is designed to
simulate with bands or blending of blue/pink/green
and gold or silver, the metallic effect achieved by Favile
glass used by Tiffany. This effect was originally developed to reproduce the oxidation found on antique
glass excavated from Roman times. Modern glass manufacturers have their own versions of the iridescent
effect, and apply it to cathedral, opalescent and occasionally, glue chip glass.

**Tiger Lily**
John and Pat Daley,
J&P Stained Glass,
Scarborough, ME
Wall mirror using
"Bullseye" glass and
separate tiger lily spot
soldered onto the frame.

**Three Apples**
John and Pat Daley,
J&P Stained Glass,
Scarborough, ME
Wall shelf mirror with
apples. Courtesy of
Mr. & Mrs. Paul Paquette,
Brunswick, ME

## Working with Mirrors

Mirror glass has its own unique history. Ancient Greek and Roman mirrors were originally thin discs of metal highly polished on one side and incised with designs, or left plain on the reverse. In the Middle Ages, glass was backed with thin sheets of steel or silver for mirrors, but in the 1500s the glassworkers of Murano blew cylinders of glass which were slit, flattened on a stone, carefully polished and the back "silvered" by an amalgam. These became the famous, unequalled Venetian mirrors until 1691 with the introduction of plate glass. Today's mirrors, with "silvering" applied as a metallic coating on glass, were not produced until 1840. Today, mirrors are available in single (1/8") or double strength (3/16") and up to 1/4" thick plate for large commercial examples.

It is this metallic coating that requires special handling when cutting and grinding. If you see an antique mirror that has black or gray spider lines and large "blots",

it's an example of "black rot". The air has gotten between the silvering and the glass, and tarnished the backing. After cutting the mirror is it very important to seal the sides of the cut with a urethane sealer or high temperature heat resistant paint (barbeque paint). This can be applied with a brush or spray-painted. Place the mirror face down on scrap paper and apply the paint to the edge of the glass and onto the back. For appearances, recommend painting the whole back of the mirror. Black backed copper foil is used on mirror to avoid reflecting the underside of the foil and will help hide any black rot that may possibly develop in the future.

Examples of rondels and pressed glass jewels.

**Quatrefoil**
Pat Daley,
Kaleidoscope Stained Glass,
Sarasota, FL

Antique glass and rondel.

## Jewels and Rondels

Another noteworthy type of glass for consideration is the availability of spun rondels and pressed glass jewels. Rondels are made by hand as a by-product of antique glass making. A gather of glass is twirled on the end of the pontil rod until gravity flattens it into a circle. After it has firmed up, it is struck from the end of the rod and allowed to continue the annealing process. Pressed jewels are made from a gather of glass that has been stamped into a "negative" steel die in the desired shape. The resulting plate of glass will have the "positive" of the jewels that will need to be cut away from the background.

There are many manufacturers of stained glass in the United States producing glass here, or moving production overseas to China. In addition, there are several distributors importing glass from Europe from well-established companies. It is recommended that each time you purchase glass, note on the sheet the maker and the glass number for future reference. Each glass is an individual entity, unique in appearance and in how it handles under cutting.

LEFT
**Pax**
Pat Daley with Harold
& Shirley Wyman,
Kaleidoscope Stained Glass,
Sarasota, FL

Peace lilies in a Moorish
"stucco wall" opening.
Antique, opal and translucent glass with a beveled
inset border.

BELOW
**Teal Spectrum Baroque
octagon window**
Pat Daley,
Kaleidoscope Stained Glass,
Sarasota, FL

Single panel, cut to fit
to let the glass "do the
work" for the design.
Commissioned by Mr.
& Mrs. William Strode,
Maggie Valley, NC.

ABOVE
**"Cool Passion" Pendant**
Pat Daley,
Kaleidoscope Stained Glass,
Sarasota, FL

A red heart fused with
dichroic blue "flame" in
center, in a gold wire wrap.

RIGHT
**Snake and Staff**
Calvin Sloan,
Star Bevel Studio,
Riverview, FL

Use of antique (back-
ground) and beveled glass.
Muted gray antique glass
accentuates the glue-
chipped golden brown
staff with beveled snake,
and wheel engraved with
a honeycomb texture.

# TOOLS AND
# THE WORKPLACE

## The Tools of the Trade

The primary tools needed to cut glass are a *glass cutter,* either straight or pistol grip handle, *score runners, breaker* or *breaker/grozier combination pliers,* ultra fine tip waterproof marker, *white* pen for dark glass, ruler, *bench brush* and paper for your pattern. Straight edge guides such as ruler or yardstick can help assure even edges to all square and rectangular shapes. Additional mechanical help is available in tabletop grinders and band saws.

To assemble the cut and ground glass pieces into your design there are two basic methods. First, the traditional method of window construction is with lead came which is soldered only at the joining intersections of lead, then cemented with glazing putty. You will need a *spring-loaded bench vise* to hold the lead for stretching and a pair of *lead nippers* or *lead knife* for cutting the came. Second, the newer (about 100 years old) technique is to use copper foil to *enfold the glass edges* and this requires soldering every bit of copper. Both methods employ the use of an *electric solder iron* (80 or 100 watts preferred), a temperature rheostat for the iron, a blend of tin and lead in ratios of 50/50 or 60/40 (the percentage of tin is listed first)

or lead-free *solder.* For both techniques, use a water-soluble flux, flux brush and container, and #000 grade steel wool or a small wire brush—never use a *rosin core solder.*

The expensive part of working with glass is the initial purchase of a glass grinder with diamond bits. Replacement bits are expensive but only needed when the glass begins to grind slowly and you find yourself pushing harder with little result. Choices abound in retail shops among 4 different manufacturers for bits. A diamond blade band saw is a nice convenience for that "piece" you must avoid breaking, or the cut that is impossible to do naturally with a cutter and grinder. This machine too is an expensive part of your tool kit, and does not replace the diamond bit grinder.

**A word about the tools**—if you purchase an *oil feed cutter,* the wheel will last longer as it is automatically lubricated when used, adjustable metal jaw *running pliers* will outlast lightweight plastic, and two pair of *breaker grozier pliers* will save your fingers and knuckles on smaller, delicate-sized breaks of glass. The grinder has become almost indispensable now in studios and saws are gaining rapid acceptance too. If

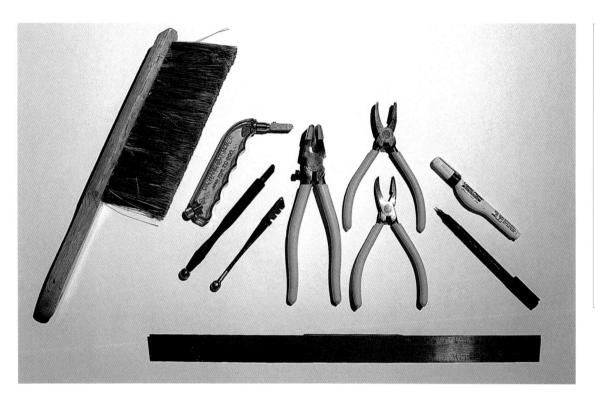

**from left
to right**
Basic Stained
Glass Tools:

1. Bench brush
2. Glass cutters
a. pistol grip
b. straight barrel
   (oil fed)
c. #o7 straight
   cutter
3. Adjustable
   metal score
   runners
4. Breaker/grozier
   plyers
5. White marker
   and black
   ultra-fine pen
6. Cork back
   metal ruler

you think working in stained glass is something you find relaxing, enjoyable, and fulfilling, then the initial expense in purchasing good tools will be outweighed by the pleasure you will have working with glass.

The basic supplies that will be consumed working with glass are less costly compared to the tools, and you will have enough for multiple projects. In the traditional lead, lengths of **H** and **U** shaped extruded lead are sized just less than 6 feet. Depending on the different sizes needed and complexity of the pattern, several lengths of lead came are not uncommon. Adhesive backed copper foil comes only in 36 foot long rolls, and the wide variety of widths and backing will mean you will acquire a collection of these quickly. The solder flux will last several projects unless you over apply the flux or have baptized the tabletop. Solder is the most consumed item in the copper foil technique

compared to its use with lead came. Patinas to color the lead, and cleaning solutions are second and third in degree of use.

The most important part of the equation is the glass and it will vary the most in quantity and price. No matter how many pieces of glass you have—*it's simply not quite the right one or the right size!* If you hoard your scrap pieces (as the author does), you will soon be overwhelmed. If the glass piece is unique or costly—yes, hold on to it, otherwise if it's less than 2"x 3"—simply toss it. You'll find it's difficult to part with any glass and very easy to get more.

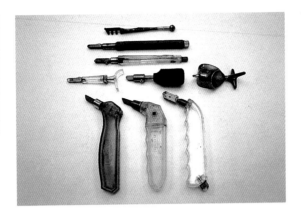

### Glass Cutters

Top Row: straight cutter with breaking notches and tapping ball.

2nd & 3rd Row: steel and plastic barrel "oil filled" cutters.

4th Row: these cutter styles are held with thumb and index finger or nestled into the palm to push or pull for scoring.

Bottom Row: three different pistol grip oil filled cutters.

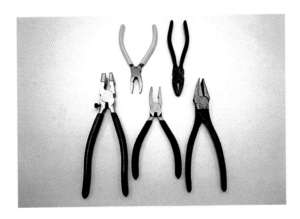

### Breakers, Breaker/Groziers and Runners

Top Row: jaw breaker/groziers and medium breakers.

Bottom Row: adjustable runners, medium breaker/groziers and wide jaw breakers.

### Lead Nippers and Cutting Knives

Lead nippers also called lead dykes, and three styles of lead cutting knives.

The advent of "hot glass" is creating a new level of glass crafting that was originally limited to specialty glass workers, such as the *glass painters* in professional studios, "lamp work" (creating figures with glass rods) and traditional glass blowers. These craftsmen used kilns and open flame in a variety of ways to produce their glasswork. Now there are a range of kilns with small 6" square beehive-shaped firing chambers for rapid firing to kilns that are shallow but up to 6' long and 2' wide. These are enjoying popularity for fusing glass, painting with enamels or glass paint, slumping or draping with pre-made molds, and adding all these special effects to stained glass work.

Other useful tools you will find necessary but not directly related to stained glass are: a woodworker's combination square and carpenter's right angle, hacksaw and miter box. These will assure that the project is squarely built and be an aid in framing with U channel. A source of copper wire can be found in 14 and 12 gauge three-way wire with ground and wire strippers from the hardware store's electrical supply department. This, then, can be used to make loops for hanging projects, and twisted copper wire makes an added decorative touch. From a jewelry supplier, a pair of large, round (cone) nose pliers will be helpful in shaping round rings of copper for making hanging loops and decorative wirework. A mini pipe or tube cutter can be used in cutting tube for hinge knuckles, and a glazing hammer and horseshoe nails for securing lead came. An anvil or antique flat iron makes a good rigid surface in using a ball peen hammer for metal work, or a solid block of lead for soft-shaping sheet copper.

At this point, it's timely to consider the use of **safety equipment**. Always wear eye protection in the form of safety goggles designed to prevent glass chips from flying into your eyes. This can happen while breaking glass or using the grinder. In addition, a plastic or glass grinder shield will help reduce the possibility of eye injury.

Fumes from heated flux and melting solder are unhealthy to inhale. The fumes carry particles of lead and if inhaled can transfer from the lungs into the blood stream. It is imperative that adequate ventilation is available. There are air filters/fans that will draw the fumes and cleanse the air. Use a paper facemask especially if you are working in a smaller space or are not near a window. If you have worked with glass for a number of years, plan to add a *lead level blood test* to your yearly physical. If you are female and planning a pregnancy stop working with lead immediately, as it will transfer through your blood to your offspring. Once you have your baby, continue to avoid lead until natural feeding is completed as mother's milk can also pass lead on. If you have the urge to cut glass, it's an ideal time to work in mosaics.

Flux is a chemical that will clean the copper foil or lead came in preparation for solder. It is a slightly mild corrosive and some people who have sensitive skin may experience a reaction such as itching or chapped hands. After soldering, immediately wipe the remaining flux residue from the glass to reduce your exposure. Latex gloves are also suggested to protect your hands. Thus, the same caution applies when using patina solutions as Latex protects your fingers from the "hot" sensation of patina or from flux entering skin cuts. Washing your hands often will help avoid these problems. In the end, glass crafting can be enjoyed for many years with the proper tools and employing safe work habits.

## Your Workspace and Work Habits

That so many people start glasswork on their kitchen counters or dining room tables, it's a wonder their families don't have glass chips in their breakfast cereal. If you are limited on space and have to work in food preparation areas, please be extremely careful about cutting glass and using chemicals. Clean the floor carefully and wash the countertops with soap to remove all chemicals when you stop working. If you have the luxury of extra space in your home, such as a spare bedroom or a space in the cellar, recommend you set up shop there.

from top
to bottom
Scissors
Soldering Irons,
Tips & Stand,
Rheostat
Other Handtools
for Stained Glass

**Scissors**
Examples of scissors used to cut the lead heart away on the paper pattern. A double blade with adjustable width is pulled on the pattern to cut; blunt-end pattern scissors have a center blade to separate the center of the pattern for the heart, and scissors with an interchangeable blade for a copper foil "heart," as well as lead.

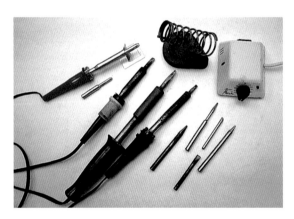

**Soldering Irons**
80 and 100-watt soldering irons with a variety of soldering tips. Accessories include iron stand and temperature rheostat control.

**Other Handtools for Stained Glass**
Hand tools that will be useful in crafting stained glass.

21

Having natural light benefits working with glass, especially when placing your pattern piece on the right spot on the sheet of glass. A bedroom windowsill will serve to prop the glass against the sash. Cellar lighting can be spotty, but can be acceptable. A light table—a pair of light bulbs in a framed wood box covered with a frosted smooth glass top—will also substitute nicely. These options are now commercially available, if you choose not to build one.

The worktable surface should be about between 32" and 36" high, depending on your height and preference. A surface can be as big as 8' by 4' or as small as 6' by 3'. It all depends on your available space and if you need to have the grinder or other items on it. Plywood with a 1/4" luan cover is an excellent surface as it may be necessary to occasionally nail into it, handle melted solder or absorb flux spills. It should be positioned where you will have good ventilation for soldering—near a window that can be opened or have a fan placed on the table. You will need electrical outlets for a rheostat, grinder, fan, extra lighting—as needed, and for radio/CD player/tape or TV, your electronic companion. A power strip with shut-off switch is a good choice and an added safety check to ensure everything is properly turned off, including hot solder-

ing irons, before leaving the area. A carpet remnant makes standing easier, can save a piece of dropped glass and protect the floor against splats and burns of dripping solder. A comfortable stool is an appropriate choice when you can sit to foil or design a project.

When planning your glass storage area, ask your glass retailer for empty crates. You can stand up glass sheets in them for storage, and placing a board on top will give you extra shelf space. Keep a wastebasket and bench brush nearby for cleaning the tabletop and discarding broken glass. Many communities recycle so consider this option with your discarded materials.

Water is necessary to clean the glass after grinding and for cleaning the finished piece. A laundry sink with spray hose or a trip to the bathtub (with a protective rubber mat) is an option, but be careful in handling your project against the sides of the sink or tub. If the project is too big, a tabletop sponge bath is the next best thing.

When working with lead and chemicals it is vital that you do not eat—touching food while working will inevitably transfer the lead or flux to it. The same concern exists with cigarette smoking—bringing your hands to your face and mouth. The key is to wash your hands thoroughly with soap before handling anything exclusive of your glasswork. Dress sensible, long pants protect against glass splinters, and avoid open-toed shoes or sandals when handling or cutting glass.

If children visit your workspace, keep the chemicals out of their reach on a shelf. Especially with young children present, you should handle all pieces of glass. These practical, common sense safety precautions will make working with glass enjoyable for all.

**from top to bottom**
Glass Grinders
Glass Saws
In-home Kilns

**Glass Grinders**
Glass grinders with diamond coated bits.

**Glass Saws**
The flat and onmi-directional diamond blade band saws.

**Kilns**
In-home, studio-sized table kilns from Paragon and Jen-Ken.

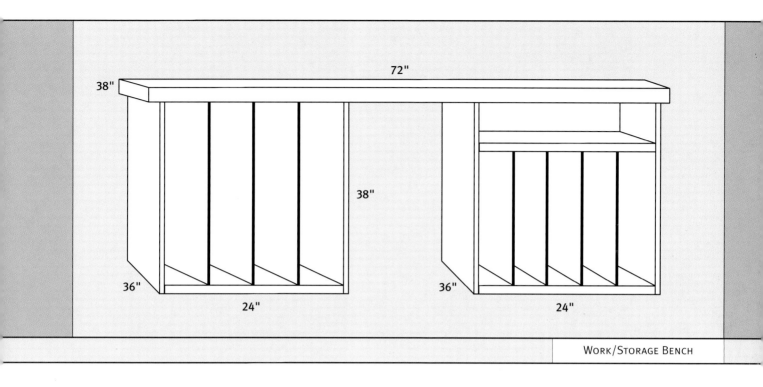

## Stained Glass Storage Bench

This layout of a workbench features storage for sheet glass in a variety of sizes and a shelf for keeping extra solder, tools and other supplies. The table top is 38" wide by 72" long using 3/4" thick plywood edged with 1 x 2 molding and covered with a commercial counter-top material. This fits down over the top of two freestanding bases.

The two bases are made with 5/8th inch plywood measuring 38" high and 24" wide by 36" deep. The single bin on the left can hold sheet glass up to 35" x 36," and the bin on the right can hold smaller pieces. The size of the glass to be held is determined by the placement of the shelf inside the bin. Supporting dividers to hold the glass can be made of 3/8th inch plywood. The dividers are placed in "rabbet" grooves made in the top and bottom of the single bin. The bottom and under the shelf of the second base, are also grooved to hold the dividers secure.

The two bases have a 1/4" luan panel-back applied to the outside edges for stability. Recommend assembly to be done with screws going into pre-drilled pilot holes to avoid splitting the wood while aiding in disassembling if the workbench needs to be relocated.

When this bench was in use in a second bedroom, we had placed one end against the wall by a window and 3' out parallel with an interior wall enabling use on both sides. A shelf with the TV was on the wall above it, and under it, a board with copper foil rolls hung by size. The power-strip rested on the bench top by the wall and the grinder stand was in the corner. Two rheostats, grinder, TV and clamp-on lighting were plugged in. The floor kiln was in another corner by a window; the shelving with books and kiln molds. A 32-drawer cabinet was in the remaining corner to hold scrap glass and patterns. The "glass room" was 10' x 11' but comfortable in which to work.

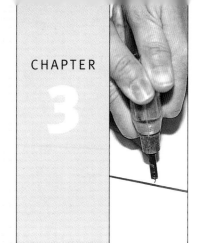

# Learning to score and break glass

With the workspace set up, tools are laid on the bench and start with a 12" x 12" piece of clear window glass for practice. If your workbench is natural wood, recommend placing your glass on top of a white paper in order to see your lines easier on the glass surface. White Kraft paper or large poster boards (found in art supplies) can be picked up to tip glass shards into a waste bin and it can used several times until flux or patina wet it.

*(Author's note: The photo examples in this chapter show the use of a pistol grip cutter and that I am left handed, but the pistol grip is ambidextrous. If you have a straight cutter please grip it either as "a pencil" or with both hands and push away from your body to follow along.)*

1. On the clear glass, draw 3 straight lines with a ruler about 1/2" apart from top to bottom. Run a dotted line between two solid lines. Next to this group, draw 3 long wavy lines from top to bottom about 1/2" apart. Again, run a dotted line between two solid lines as in the photo. Draw a straight line next to the wavy grouping as a base to draw the inside curves and half circle, as in the example.

## Straight Lines

2. Grasp the cutter firmly and place the cutter wheel about 1/8" in, from the edge of the glass. Proceed to exert a moderate downward pressure on the head of the cutter using your forearms and wrists as you push it along the thin solid line. You will hear a "skritch" or crunching sound as the wheel moves on the glass. When you reach the end of the line, lift up about 1/8" before you go off the edge of the glass. Then take a deep breath. You'll discover you will hold your breath while scoring glass.

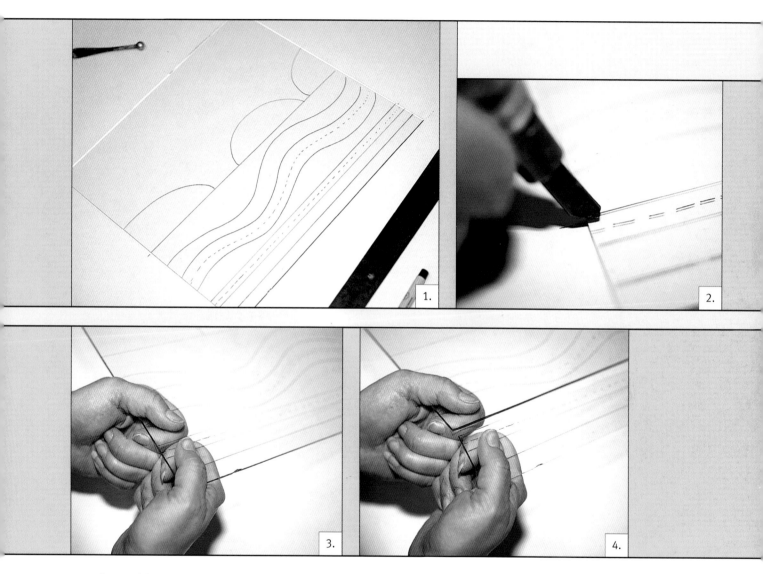

## Hand Breaking

3. To break the glass by hand, position your thumbs on or about 1/8" on either side of the score and curl your index fingers under your thumbs as in the photo. Your other fingers will be curled tightly together.

4. Move one wrist pulling a clenched hand downward and apart, starting from the thumb and spreading down to your "pinkie" finger. When you pull one hand downward, the glass will break upward from underneath the score and snap off from the rest of the sheet. If you have trouble with one hand, try moving both wrists together in opposite directions and it will break.

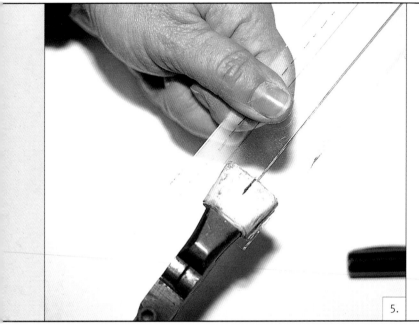

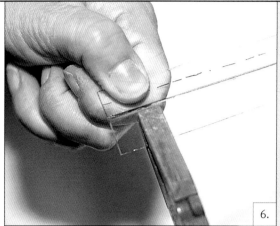

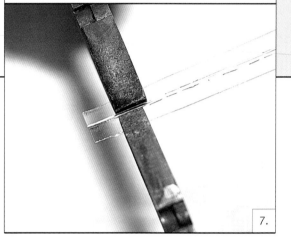

## Using Runners and Breakers

5. Score the next solid line from the original edge of the glass. Take the adjustable running pliers (called "runners") and examine them. Open the "jaws" and note that the bottom one is a convex curve, and the top section matches with a concave shape. Glass, as you have learned in the hand-break method, breaks upward from underneath the score. The outside, downward curve of the top jaw forces the bottom curve upward, centering on the score. The same action occurs when your thumbs apply downward force while your curled fingers underneath bring upward pressure on the score. The screw on the pliers indicates the top of the runners and a centerline on the top jaw. Line this up in the direction of the score and seat the glass into the jaws, almost all the way in. Gently squeeze the pliers and the glass score will break.

6. Try the breaker/grozier pliers next by scoring one of the solid lines next to the dotted line. The breaker pliers have a pincher appearance similar to oversized tweezers. Both jaws are widely spaced in the back to accommodate the thickness of the glass but close at the front and are flat surfaced. The breaker/grozier combination pliers have a lower curved jaw and a straight upper jaw with file-like serrations lining both. To snap the glass with breakers, place the flat jaw beside the score about 1/16" away. Close the jaws firmly and hold the glass with thumb and curled fingers on the opposite side of the score. Your hand remains still while resting on the table. Then, pull downward with the breakers to snap the glass off to the side away from your hand.

7. If you have two-pair of breaker pliers, you can score the dotted line and place the two pair on either side of the score, "nose-to-nose" with flat jaws on top. Snap upwards in the same motion as a hand break. The tools become an extension of your hands and fingers in making narrow strips of glass.

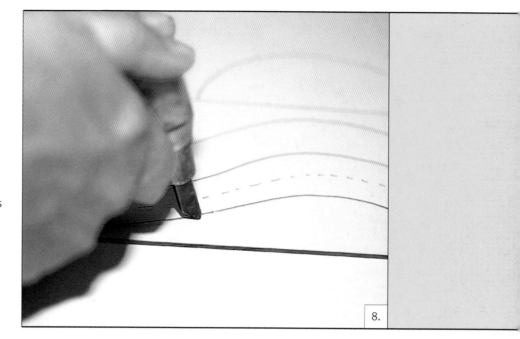

8.

## Wavy Lines

8.  Scoring a wavy line is simple as long as you focus on the wheel on the line, avoid excessive lean of the cutter, left or right. Move your body to follow the line keeping the cutter upright and firm from your forearms to the wrists.

9.  You can run the score with the running pliers but because of the curve, the run may not go all the way to the farther edge. In the photo look for the shiny break at the end of the runners and follow it almost out of frame where it darkens and ends on the scored line. Carefully rotate the glass sheet and run the score from the opposite end to meet the break.

10. If this does not occur, move the sheet to the edge of the table and grasp the side near the break with the breaker pliers, flat jaw on top. Slide the glass so the breaking section of glass will be off the table. Pull downward with the breaking pliers to finish the separation off the table.

11. If you do not have running pliers but can come close to the score "sideways" with the breakers, slight downward pressure applied beside the score, moving down the length of the score, will also run the glass. Try this on the next part of the wave group on a solid line. Separate the wave with the dotted centerline next, and score the centerline. If you have two breakers, work your way up with opposing breakers "nose-to-nose", up the length until it separates.

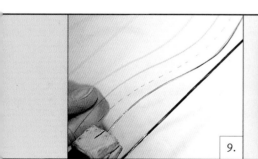

9.

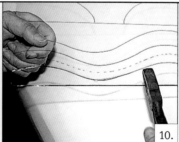

10.

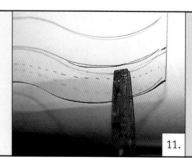

11.

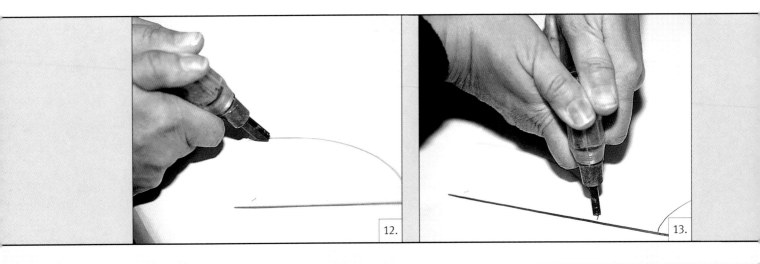

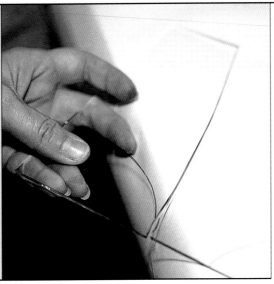

If the end of the score is not deep enough, the glass will not break correctly as seen here.

## Half Round Curves

12. Since you have become comfortable with the tools, it's time to do the half-round and long curves. It's best to test the position with a dry run pass of the cutter just to get the feel of it. Position the glass so the straighter part of the curve is tight to you—at first it may seem awkward to seat the cutter on the glass so close to the body at a slightly twisted angle. However, as you go into the curve, straighten your position up to the table.

13. The final hook of the line will not be difficult to achieve as you can comfortably reach it with the cutter. If you are still "corkscrewed" at the bend in the line, move the glass so it's tougher to start, but you will have body weight for score pressure as you slowly move the cutter on the line and swivel your shoulders and upper arms to follow the cutter. Partially break it from either edge with the runners by gently squeezing until the breaks meet.

14. Continue with the remaining two practice shapes on the glass. Notice the starting point position of the hand in the photo example for the half circle, then at the half point, and almost to the end of the line. Soon you will recognize you cut best from one direction over another for circles or long curves. The finish of the half circle is the breaking from both ends using the runner pliers.

14.

**Reading your cutting pressure by examining the edge of the glass.** Tilt and closely examine the edge of the glass until the light highlights the tiny "scratches" along of the edge where the cutter wheel was used. These marks are important as they indicate how much force you are exerting to score the glass. The wheel creates a groove in the surface to "divide" the glass, not to physically cut as a saw goes through wood. You can have too much pressure crushing the glass as the wheel passes over it, or if too light, little or no impression is made. The heavy pressure shows large splinters along the score and that will reflect on the break edge displaying jagged, uneven markings up and down the thickness of the glass. Lack of pressure or skips in pressure will cause the glass to break in an uncontrolled manner—if at all as shown in the photo for the long curve at the finish end. Good, consistent pressure will show as even markings on the break edge of the glass going no deeper than almost half the thickness. Some glass requires scoring with slightly heavier pressure in order to break, but the average piece prefers proper cutting techniques. The resulting edge of the glass will determine if you need to groze or grind the glass in order to fit it to your pattern piece.

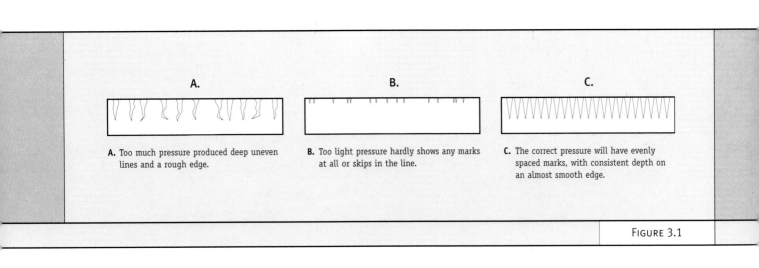

**A.** Too much pressure produced deep uneven lines and a rough edge.

**B.** Too light pressure hardly shows any marks at all or skips in the line.

**C.** The correct pressure will have evenly spaced marks, with consistent depth on an almost smooth edge.

FIGURE 3.1

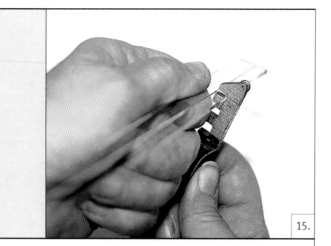

## Using a Straight Cutter

15. If you are using a straight cutter from the hardware store, there are different sized notches near the wheel and a small ball at the other end. You can use the notch or grozing teeth to slip over the edge of the glass beside the score, and use as a lever to snap-off the small point of glass or narrow strip in the same way as with the breaking pliers. However, the depth of the notch will not be useful on scores beyond 1/2", therefore, it is rarely used.

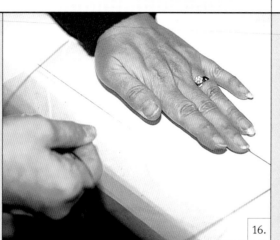

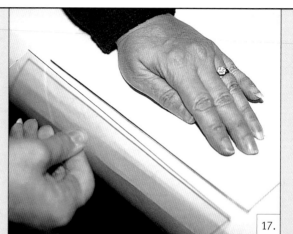

## Table Snap

16. Place the glass so the score is suspended about 1/4" beyond the table edge. Place one hand at opposite glass edge—half on the glass—half flat on the table.

17. With your other hand firmly grasping the suspended edge, raise the glass to pivot on the edge under your hand and bring it smartly downward, "slapping it" on the tabletop. This will snap only straight lines of any length.

## Grozing

18. Grozing is the snipping and chewing of glass off the sheet to reach the score or to finish removing small portions that occur with intersecting scores. The curved jaw of the breaker/grozier pliers is placed on top of the glass at about a 45° angle and only 1/8" onto the glass itself. Only the corner of the jaws is used to snip with a moderate downward pressure similar to cutting with scissors. Larger bites are used to chew and pull the glass away when near the score line. Again, this will leave a very jagged edge and will need to be ground.

## Tapping

19. The small ball on the end of a straight cutter is used to "tap" underneath the score to cause it to break within a very short radius of the strike. Moving and tapping the ball underneath the score creates a series of "intermittent breaks" to separate the glass from the sheet.

20. The edge of this method will be jagged and sharp as shown in the "how to" example of the wave score.

21. To summarize the three methods of breaking a score line, look at the photo example with a half-round curve. The first score to the edge has been grozed, the middle score has been tapped with the ball, and the final inside score is run with runners or gentle side pressure with breakers.

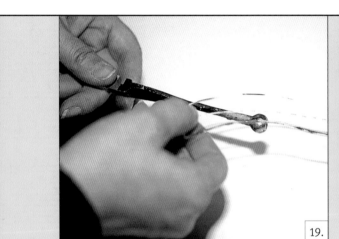

19.

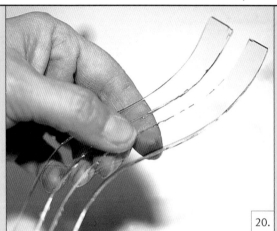

20.

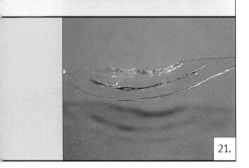

21.

## Final words on scoring and breaking glass:

A. All lines that make up a piece to be cut will be combinations of straight, wavy or curved lines.

B. All scores must start from one edge of the glass and continue to another edge. There is no starting or stopping in the middle of the sheet.

C. Do not lift the cutter while you are scoring, otherwise you will have a difficult time finding the end point to restart, and could break the sheet incorrectly when separating your piece out.

D. Score lines may intersect at any point but never run the cutter in the same score twice as the glass will not know how you want it to separate and will break in an uncontrollable manner.

E. It is not possible to cut a right angle in glass without losing the sheet. (Unless you resort to the use of a band saw).

F. Have a healthy respect for glass as it is sharp and will cut your skin. Wear safety glasses as appropriate and have a first aid kit at hand.

CHAPTER
4

# DESIGNING a PROJECT anD SELECTING THE GLASS

Having accomplished cutting window glass, you are ready to start cutting real stained glass. There is still the planning stage to consider—what to make? There are a wide variety of pattern books available on any subject and any degree of complexity. These resources provide an appropriate starting point for creative inspiration along with the many images in your environment ...a tree beside a stone wall...a group of flowers in a vase, birds or whatever attracts you and brings enjoyment can be a subject for stained glass design.

If you are a beginner, you can draw your own patterns by keeping in mind a few simple rules.

**A.** Start with a simple, realistic size. A beginner's starting panel should be at most 1 to 2 square feet. It will be more rewarding than a "sun catcher" in that you will have had to make decisions on glass color and placement, and not without a fair amount of time and effort.

**B.** A balanced design will make the eye travel in a circle, triangle or square around the entire panel assessing all the parts.

**C.** Color in your drawing to see what it will look like. This exercise will help you select glass.

**Pineapple**
Pat Daley,
Kaleidoscope Stained Glass, Sarasota, FL
Commissioned by William Dunn, Sarasota, FL

**D.** Check your design to see if there are any impossible glass piece cuts, and that the lines flow naturally to the edge of the glass.

**E.** Decide what method of construction will be used to make this project—traditional lead came or copper foil. Either method has advantages and limitations and should be considered in terms of your pattern choice.

**F.** Vary the width of your lines to create depth of field or use them as an effect such as in vines or leaves. Changes in the sizes of foil or lead will physically accomplish this desirable effect as you are building your project.

**G.** If the design has too many small pieces, while much detail is displayed, the effect of the glass color/ direction may be lost. Start with simple ideas, moderate sized pieces and let the glass do the work, then experiment with adding extra shading or more complex lines with related glass colors.

**H.** If you do use pattern books, know you may see the same (book) item made by someone else, but yours will be different because of your choice of glass and color.

The final drawing should be rendered in ink with all the pieces numbered, and then add any directional marks or shading cues. Have a photocopy or carbon copy made on heavier paper (67# or 80# weight) from which to cut the pattern pieces. The original design or a copy will be used to position the glass pieces for assembly.

ABOVE
**Hoppin' John Pirate Window (detail)**
Seymour & Anita Isenberg, From the author's personal collection.

An example of using different width lines to show depth. The straight and diamond window panes are done in copper foil and the window sash is made with wider, flat lead came.

ABOVE
**Ribbon and Roses**
Pat Daley, Kaleidoscope Stained Glass, Sarasota, FL
Curving lines flow from tips of leaves to edge. Commissioned by Lisa and Scott Costello, North Port, FL

LEFT
**Wild Iris**
John and Pat Daley, J&P Stained Glass, Scarborough, ME
Book pattern from "Flowers of the Field" with John's choice of Youghiogheny glass and use of decorative wave copper foil. Wyman Residence, Bradenton, FL

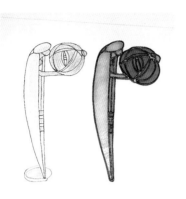

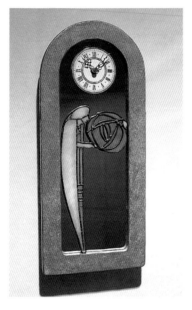

ABOVE
**Lady with Rose Clock**
Pat Daley,
Kaleidoscope Stained Glass,
Sarasota, FL

Leaded figure used as focal
point on mirror clock design.

TOP RIGHT
**Victorian Half-round
Transom Window**
From the author's personal
collection.

Antique lead came window
using textured cathedral
glass. Made in the late 1800s.

## Design and Choosing Glass

After you are satisfied with the design and made the appropriate copies,
you choose the glass. Whatever color or texture you select, you will need
to look at the glass to determine the right spot for a particular piece of
the pattern. Use your imagination to visualize the "brushstroke" in
opalescent or the shading in antique mouth blown glass. Textured glass
can give an extra depth to a flat panel, as granite or ripple can indicate
water, tree bark, rocks, shapes in clothing or be used as an overall
background—the possibilities are endless. Geometric designs can be
accentuated with textured pieces as part of the overall panel. This wide
variety of choices can be compared to a painting of a subject in heavy oil
paint or with the more delicate feeling of a watercolor. The same glass
design will have a different appearance done in antiques and cathedrals
(with or without textured surfaces) compared to unaltered or textured
opalescent. The sooner you recognize the different types of manufactured
glass, and that while the color formulas are similar, you will see that the
density and evenness of the color mix in the finished sheet vary by
maker. As an example, one manufacturer will produce a two color
opalescent glass that will distribute the colors so uniformly on the sheet,
that if a repair is necessary, the new piece will match the broken one.
Conversely, another manufacturer may have areas that are predominately
one color over the second in various places in the sheet, and a broken
piece may require the task of looking at several sheets to find a match for
an exact replacement. Glass sample boxes can be misleading. What looks
fantastic as a 2" by 3" sample of art glass, may not even appear on the
whole sheet when seen at a distributor or retailer, even though you have
referenced it by the manufacturer's number. Knowing the design you have
in mind, choose the glass, gauge what effect your design requires when
working with opalescent, and carefully move the glass to determine the
range of pieces available.

**Hummingbird
& Morning Glory**
Pat Daley,
Kaleidoscope Stained Glass,
Sarasota, FL

Antique window sash
saved from family
home and refurbished.
Commissioned by Susan
Hess, Sarasota, FL.

ABOVE
**Native American-style Panel**
Pam Bowditch,
Sarasota, FL

Variety of color selected in
Spectrum waterglass and use
of spun rondels and pressed
square jewel.

ABOVE
**Mike's Bi-Plane**
Pat Daley,
Kaleidoscope Stained Glass,
Sarasota, FL

A gift for a family member
who used to fly in the
1930s from Bigg's Field, PA.
Commissioned by
Frank Guididras.

LEFT
**Nude**
Calvin Sloan,
Star Bevel Studio,
Riverview, FL

Simple line design gives an
elegant shape to this figure
and the use of a "fracture"
or "confetti" glass shows
texture in the robe without
requiring additional cuts.

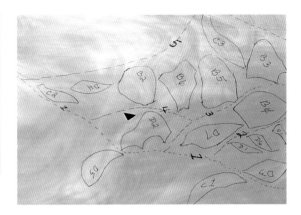

With the glass in your work area, you are ready to cut the heavy paper pattern into the individual pieces. If you are using lead came, use the lead scissors; the copper foil method has scissors available too. I have found in grinding, the excess is removed. Accordingly, these can be grouped by the subject of your design or by color for ease. Now that the pattern pieces are loose, the helpful hints of shading or by following the direction of the "grain" will assist you in placing them on glass for tracing. Place the pattern pieces in from the edge about 1/8" allowing you to seat the cutter before following the line. Look for any special markings in the glass that will enhance that piece, a swirl in the glass to indicate veins in a leaf or the shadings of a rose petal, regardless of where it may be on the sheet.

Resist placing all the same color pattern pieces in a row just to save opalescent or textured glass, or the finished project will show that no effort was made to give the glass movement or life. Only in using smooth cathedral or new antique glass, where the distinguishing grain and shadings are missing, should the pieces be lined up for row cutting.

1. Position space between each piece to gain a place for the runner or breakers to hold the glass. If you have arranged all your pieces and traced them, number them with the matching pattern number before cutting.

2. Look at the marked sheet and plot a course through the maze you have drawn on the glass. Score the path of least resistance to isolate groups of pieces; by doing this you minimize the possible loss of the balance of the sheet by exposing a flaw in the glass or executing a bad score. Then cut these groups down to the individual pieces.

3. Grind, rinse and dry the glass before fitting it to your paper pattern for reassembly.

**Master Bedroom Window**
Pat Daley,
Kaleidoscope Stained Glass, Sarasota, FL
Based on a Clarice Cliff design from
English pottery "Bizarreware" with
customer color preferences. Commisioned by
Mr. & Mrs. William Strode, Maggie Valley, NC.

ABOVE LEFT
**Oriental Tree**
Jan Stratton, Pennsylvania
Round panel, an effective use
of calming soft blue/purple.
The detail is an intricate cut
for blossoms into background
glass and a flow of lines for
hanging blooms. Courtesy of
Mr. Robert Roggio, Sarasota, FL.

ABOVE RIGHT
**Oriental Swan**
Jan Stratton, Pennsylvania
Round panel companion to
"Oriental Tree" with bamboo
and irises. Detail shows excel-
lent use of Bullseye glass to
shade the swan's body and
feathers with variations within
the single piece of glass.
Courtesy of Mr. Robert Roggio,
Sarasota, FL.

LEFT
**Blue Agate panel**
Shirley Wyman,
Bradenton, FL
The *blue agate slice* is
a focal point in this
abstract design.

*The following chapter deals with
"how to solder" which will need to
be addressed before proceeding to
your choice of the two techniques:
building your design with either
lead came or copper foil.*

# THE BASICS OF SOLDERING

The craft of stained glass is defined by three distinct steps in fabricating a project—regardless of whether it is a flat panel, lampshade or dimensional piece such as a box or free-form sculpture. The cutting of glass is the first, building a framework of lead or wrapping with copper foil to hold the glass is second, and the final assembly joining it all together with solder making it a solid. Lead came is wrapped and fitted to the glass and joints. It is closed with solder at the intersections and at abutting lead; conversely, copper foil is completely covered with solder. The fine art of soldering is not difficult if proper techniques are learned in the beginning. Photographs of these processes are detailed within the following chapters.

The tools for both methods are the same except copper foil does not require a wire brush.

**Soldering tools** (clockwise from left to right)
1. Rheostat temperature control
2. Water-soluable flux
3. Solid core solder
4. 100-watt solder iron with stand
5. Flux brush and dish
6. #000 grade steel wool

## Soldering for the Lead Came Method

1. Rub the joint of the lead came with a wire brush or steel wool to clean any oxidation from the surface of the lead.

2. Dip the flux brush into the flux and stroke the brush where you cleaned the came.

3. Take the soldering iron and 60/40 solder spool, and place the solder wire on the flat side of the tip of the iron. The solder will melt onto the tip.

4. Place the hot iron tip lightly where the came intersects and allow the solder to flow from the tip onto the seam where the came meet. The solder will puddle on the one spot on the seam.

5. To distribute solder across the joint place the iron tip directly beside it, the heat will draw the solder to it, and flow where the came was fluxed. Do this immediately to the left and right of the joint and only the width of the iron tip for a neat seam. A smooth solder joint on lead will be almost even with the top of the came. If the came was cut slightly short, add a sliver of came without the heart to fill the gap and cover with solder as above. Too much heat from a soldering iron can melt a piece of lead came, necessitating its replacement.

6. Turn the panel over and repeat the steps above to solder the backside.

For this method, I recommend 60/40 solder as it melts quickly and stays liquid longer to flow onto the came.

## Soldering in the Copper Foil Method

1.

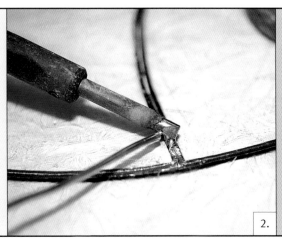

2.

For this method, I recommend using 50/50 solder for learning purposes, as it solidifies quickly and results in faster work on dimensional projects too.

1. Assemble the foiled pieces together on the paper pattern and hold in position with tape or push pins if needed. Flux by applying a quick brush stroke to the copper foil in the approximate center of the edge of a piece of glass. Melt a small amount of solder on the tip of the iron and place the tip of the iron on the copper foil to allow the solder to flow onto the foil. This will "spot tack" the pieces together to hold them for soldering and you may remove any pins or tape holding the glass in position.

2. Flux with a longer stroke along the copper foil, beginning with one end of the line going to an intersection.

**Pendulum**
Harold Wyman,
Bradenton, FL

Abstract panel using
antique pressed
jewels, bevels and
textured glass.

3.  Melt the solder with a cutting motion using the
    rounded side of the iron tip, and apply the solder
    continuously along the foil with the rounded part of
    the iron tip, rather than the flat. Do this for about
    an inch or two and with the iron. Double back only
    to reheat the solder to melt into a smooth rounded
    bead elevated from the surface of the glass. Then
    continue from the end where you left off applying
    more solder, and repeat.

    The solder will not stick to the glass if you drip on it
    accidentally. Do not attempt to melt the misplaced
    solder onto the tip on the glass, as this can heat-
    crack the glass causing replacement. Let it cool and
    then pick it off with a razor blade or "x-acto" knife.

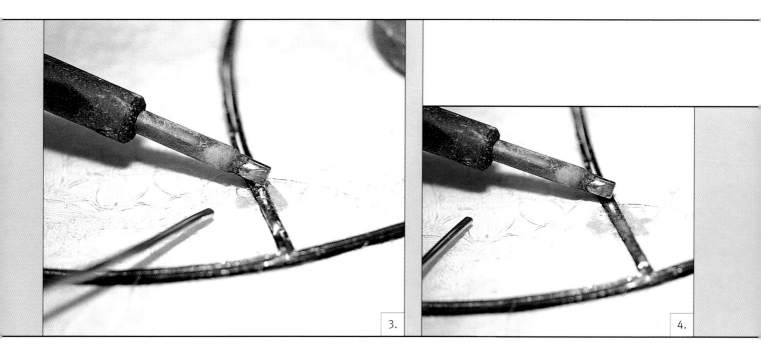

3.

4.

4.  Continue applying solder to cover all the exposed foil. If you are framing your panel with zinc, copper or brass "**U**" channel, do not solder to the very edge of the panel as you will need to fit the "**U**" channel onto the edge of the glass, then attach it by soldering from the front and back to secure it.

5.  When the first side is completed, bend down to the table-top and look across the surface of the glass and solder lines. Soldered copper foil lines are meant to imitate rounded lead came and should be evenly raised on the surface. If you see any low spots, you can go back and melt more solder onto them and blend the higher portions of solder into the existing line by heating both left and right of the area in question.

6.  Carefully, turn your panel over and continue the same process on the backside. If you "melt through" from the first side, blend that solder as you come to it. If you turn back to the first side and find melted through "mushrooms" of solder, simply blend them in.

5.

Everyone does unintentional "decorative" soldering in the beginning, but with practice, smooth solder joints can be easily accomplished. Properly soldered joints are the key to hold the glass pieces together while giving strength to the panel, lampshade or dimensional work. Always finish the inside or backside of your work with the same care as you do on the front or outside. Decorative soldering has its place to enhance a solder line for a special effect on a dimensional piece, or as a highlight on a framed panel, for example. This is usually performed only on copper foil soldering as it can be redone. Lead came can be struck with the tip of the iron to carve a texture into the round came, but there is no way to correct a misplaced ball of solder. Various textures, balls and built up solder shapes can be melted on/into a solder line. Try experimenting with different temperatures from the rheostat to bounce the iron tip on the solder line for a dappled or scaly look. A hammered effect can be achieved by a slower touch to the line and small "pearls" can be melted from the corner tip of the iron using a tiny amount of solder onto the soldered line. As an example, large blobs of solder, of a similar type, can be added to box corners creating "feet." Anything you decide you don't like can be carefully melted away and you start over.

# reinforcing techniques

At some time, either in a church or a public building, you have seen stained glass windows that are larger than your windows at home. In looking at them, very often we are too engrossed in seeing the colors and design to be drawn to the mechanics of what is holding it up. There's a secret. Although there is external support going from left to right of the window to the frame, the eye is fooled into not seeing it. If bars are initially noticed crossing a lead window design, over time the faint shadow of the bar is taken for granted and become "invisible".

## Reinforcing Lead Came Panels

Reinforcing lead came panels and windows are very important. The general rule is any panel wider than 24" and taller than 18" to 24" needs to be reinforced on the horizontal to prevent sagging in the future. Lead stretches and keeps moving under the weight of the completed panel. Any window or panel needs to have exterior support applied 18" to 24" apart, and above the first 18" or 24" in height. If your panel is 36" tall, you need to support it at the center, here at 16". As an example: if the finished piece is 6 feet tall, you would install rebar at 24" and 48," measured from the bottom.

Steel reinforced lead is available but this is normally used in straight lines only in vertical positions. The lead has to be cut to size, then the steel cut separately, and the steel is threaded up into the opening in the heart of the came.

Copper-coated steel flat wire can be placed on both sides of the heart, in lead came, to help stiffen the came. This would be concealed inside, however, allowance needs to be made for the extra width of the heart when fitting the glass pieces. The wire would follow contours with some pre-bending into shape required—good for smaller panels.

1.

"Rebar" is an acronym for reinforcing bar. This can be a flat steel or zinc strip 1/8" thick with varying widths of 1/4" to 1" and 6' long. This can be bent with some work to follow the contour of lead lines on the horizontal. This would need to be spot soldered at even intervals across the span of the panel and anchored by notching it to fit into the wood or metal frame that will contain the work. It's required for 2' or more wide panels.

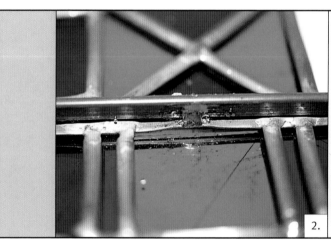
2.

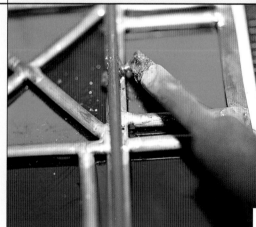
3.

**Reinforcing Bar (Rebar):**
A galvanized steel rod used to span a lead or copper foil window to prevent it from bowing.

Round rebar, found in older homes and churches, is a round steel bar that has been seated though holes in the wood sash frame with the panel itself tied to the bars. The bar is laid across the panel at the appropriate measurement and every 8" to 12" where it passes over the came, the came is marked. The bar is removed and a 14 or 12 gauge copper wire about 4" long is soldered to the came at each mark, at a 90 degree angle. The bar is replaced through the sash frame and the wire is brought up and twisted over the bar. The twisted strand is cut down to about 1 inch and folded over to one side, on top of the bar.

1. Add a drop of solder to the lead came where the flat rebar is to be affixed. Add solder to the rebar edge that will be next to the came. By priming both with solder there is less risk of melting came while trying to heat the slower, thicker rebar.
2. Position the rebar and melt the two spots of solder together.
3. Add solder to both sides of the rebar to firmly affix to the lead came.

4. Solder the copper wire firmly onto the lead came.

5. Place the round rebar into position and bring the copper wire up and around it.

6. Twist the wire tightly in place and trim it. The final step is to fold the twist down onto the rod.

5.

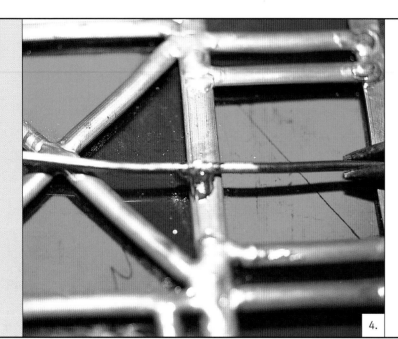

4.

6.

## Reinforcing Copper Foil Panels

Although the glass is held firmly with the adhesive foil, reinforcing is also necessary. With the copper foil method, this can be done internally in the solder line or afterwards using an external flat rebar. The internal method uses 4 types of material. The larger the span to be covered the heavier the material should be. A good rule of thumb is to go 12"–18" up any panel that is wider and/or taller than 24". It's the same as in lead came work.

**A. Copper braid**—a soft flexible braid made of fine copper strand. It is often used for solder wick—to remove unwanted solder by fluxing it, heating the solder and drawing it up onto a short length of braid. This can also be used as filler in wide gaps between the glass edges to avoid working with a large amount of liquid solder that could heat-crack the glass.

**B. Reinforcing strip**—a thin narrow strip that can slip in between the glass edges and be soldered in position. Two companies manufacture this: one is exactly 1/8" wide to fit flush with the glass, and the second is slightly wider to be higher and requires slower soldering to completely cover both foiled edges. This can be bent to follow the curves and angles exactly in the panel as seen in the following photos.

**C. Copper wire**—usually 14 or 12 gauge can be used and soldered on top of the foil. The addition of wire to the solder bead will transfer heat along the foil, but requires patience in covering it as part of the soldering process. Wire will reinforce the rim-edge of lampshades and keep tapered lamp panels from spreading apart. Lighter, thinner gauges, such as 18 and 16, can be used around delicate "sun catchers" for reinforcing glass pieces that are attached to the outside edge, without contacting one another. The higher the number of the gauge, the thinner the wire and it's less effective.

For the best results and to gain the optimum shape in "weaving" reinforcing strip or wire in the solder is in a "**T**" or "**X**" shape within the panel design, if possible. Straight lines such as water or geometric designs need stiffening with reinforcing strip or wire to help avoid a "hinging" motion. Otherwise, it weakens the soldered foil on the glass by allowing the glass to flex back and forth, and loosen the adhesive foil.

**D. Zinc coated steel rebar**—the same rebar that can be used for lead came reinforcing is applied here in the same manner. Mark where it would be attached across the solder lines. Add solder to the bar first and then contact it to the solder line on the glass panel. When working on the reverse side of a panel, support may be necessary using a shim under the edges to equal the raised area with the rebar.

**Ribbon and Roses**
Pat Daley,
Kaleidescope Stained Glass,
Sarasota, FL

Commissioned by Lisa and
Scott Costello, North Port, FL.

1. Re-strip is anchored at the edge of the glass panel.

2. Feed re-strip into the gap between the pieces.

3. Center in the gap and spot tack to hold the position.

4. Feed into corner detail. Solder up to intersection then join the lines.

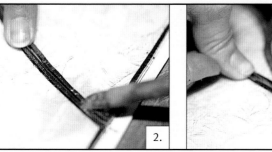

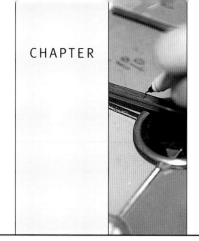

# THE TRADITIONAL LEAD CAME METHOD

This method is the centuries-old way of assembling pieces of glass into the finished works we see every day in older residences, commercial building, as well as churches. New construction is making use of glass panels built with the same method using the same extruded shapes in zinc and brass came, as well.

Came comes in various widths but the commonly used shapes are "**H**" to hold the glass and "**U**" for giving a finished edge to the overall project. The flat surface of the came is the "flange" and the short center between the flanges is the "heart". The profile of the lead came can be half round, flat or if antique, molded with raised profiles similar to wood window mullions. For long runs of came, where extra strength is required, there is a type using steel reinforcing within the heart of the lead. There are specialty shapes such as "**Y**" for holding the glass, for having a flange to nail through to a wood frame and two **U** shapes made into a 90° corner for unusual projects. Some of these same profiles are available in zinc and brass came.

1. Lead came comes in precut lengths of almost 6 feet but lead needs to be stretched to give it strength. Locate an area to do this without obstacles in the event you lose your grip or the came is over stretched and breaks, and you awkwardly step backwards. A spring-loaded came vise can be mounted at the farther end of your bench. Place an end of the came in the vise. A tap with a hammer will seat the grip teeth into the lead and hold it for pulling. At the other end of the came, firmly grasped with breaking pliers, place your foot to brace yourself and pull the came towards you. The came will resist for a moment but then you will feel it give and come to you. If you have a pre-marked 6' spot to measure against, when the came reaches that point, stop pulling. The flanges may have closed slightly tighter and may need to be opened by sliding a "lathekin" or sharpened dowel down the channel between them, near the heart.

2. Cutting the came is done either with a wide curved blade knife or with pliers called nippers or lead dykes. All cuts are made with the upper and lower flange placed next to the blade or placing cutting jaws sideways toward the heart. Note that a cut made downward from top of a flange will crush the flange and collapse the heart. A came knife must constantly be sharpened, and heavy pressure carefully applied to cut lead came.

3. The lead nippers are easier to use, as are all pliers. **Only cut lead** with them as cutting any other metal will notch the cutting portion of the jaws and this will prevent smooth butt joints. Nippers will give a straight cut on one side and a 45° point on the other as shown in the photo example. You can achieve long tapering points by placing the nippers at an exaggerated angle beside the flange.

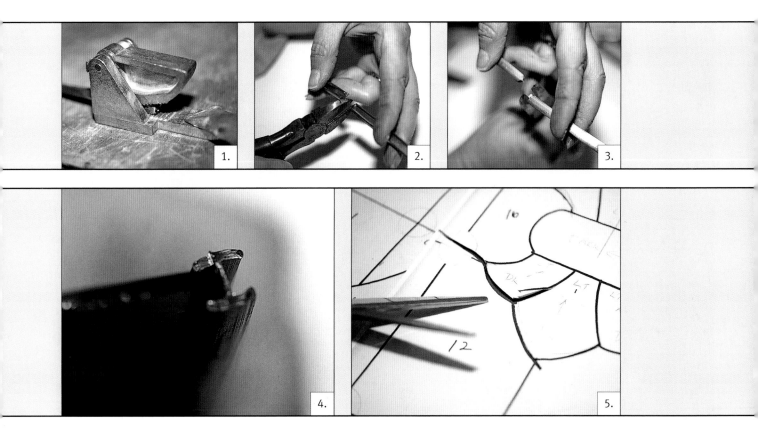

4. Special allowance for the width of the heart (in building with any type of came) has to be made when designing your project. The heart in lead came takes up about 1/8 of an inch. Each adjoining piece of glass has to be reduced about a 1/16 of an inch to fit next to the heart.

5. Pattern scissors, used to cut the paper patterns, remove the width of the heart automatically with a third blade that cuts the center out.

6. Trace the paper pattern pieces onto the glass lead panel.

7. Once the paper pattern is transferred to the glass, cutting can begin. In this particular panel, the navy blue antique mouth blown glass varied in thickness and required the use of a saw.

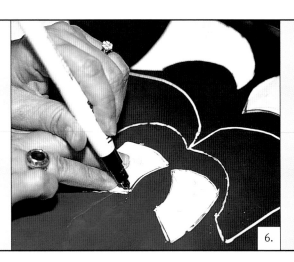

The author has previous experience cutting this "temperamental sheet." It was the only sheet on hand and the only place to position the glass pattern piece for the desired shading.

6.

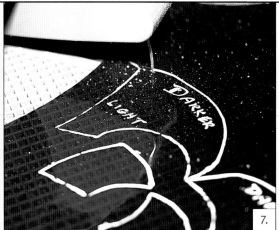

7.

8.

9.

8. When building with came, place your pattern and glass pieces on flat plywood that can be nailed to hold the pieces in position. The finished cut panel shows the space allowed for the heart before leading.

9. Gather your tools needed to lead a panel. They are the glazing hammer, lead came, nippers and horse shoe nails.

10. To start adding came, first shim and nail the glass edges with small pieces of came to raise and match the strips going in. This makes it easier to slide the strips between the glass. Use small shim pieces of came, positioned across the joint on the adjoining glass, to determine the cut length of the came. Add came up to the area where circles or curved pieces will be fitted. Secure completed areas from moving by nailing with shims against the glass or came.

11. Wrap the circles by extending the came past the starting point, mark where overlapped and cut for a butt join. Position the split at a joint for soldering.

11.

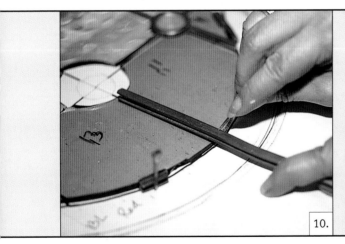

10.

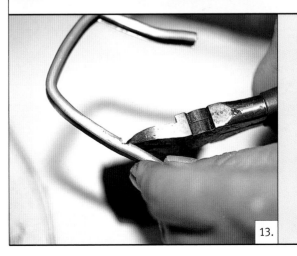

12.

12. Fit inside right angle shapes by matching the edge of the glass with a mark on the came.

13. Cut a "**V**" notch in the side of top flange to the heart and the same again, directly underneath to the bottom flange. As a result, the excess is removed and the came is to be tightly wrapped around the corner of the glass.

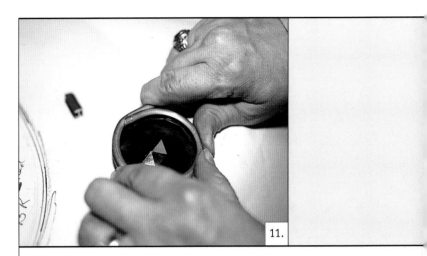

13.

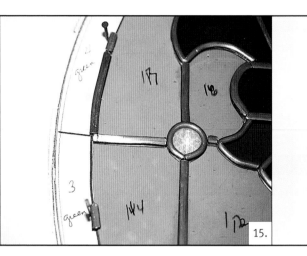

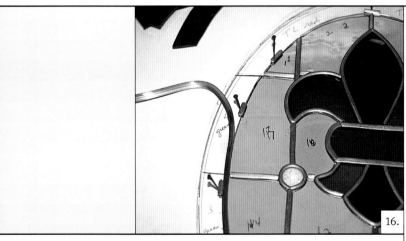

14. Position wrapped pieces in place and mark the came between them for cutting. Remove the wrapped piece and slip the came strip in position and add the wrapped piece.

15. The came, extending over the outside edge of the glass, is marked for cutting by placing a straight cut end of the appropriate came shim on the edge of the glass next to the excess on the joint. Mark and remove the piece, cut and replace it.

16. The next strip of came to be added will pass beside it with a flush fit.

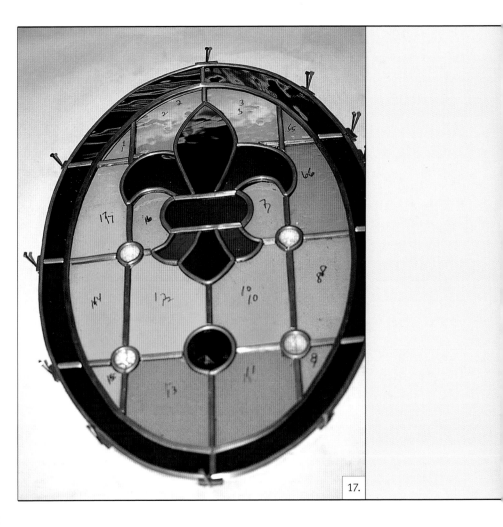

17.

17. The leaded panel is secure from movement with shim lead and nails placed around the outside edge.

Next, solder all the intersecting joints. Soldering came requires fast melting solder, 60/40 is preferred as your aim is to add the solder to the joint and not melt the lead came. To see how long this takes, place 3 square small scrap pieces of glass, two side by side and the third on top in the center over the seam. Add scrap lead to make the intersecting joint and flux. Heat the solder and let it flow onto the came. The heat from the solder will travel into the lead and let the solder flow onto it. Hold the iron longer and the came will "raggedly melt" from the thin flanges toward the heart or back from the cut end, exposing glass. Now that you have deliberately melted a joint, you have a sense of how long you can manipulate the solder on lead.

All joints need to be cleaned of any surface lead oxidation by wire brushing or using coarse steel wool. Flux the joint and add solder from the top of the iron tip so it flows down onto the lead came. Extend the solder the width of the iron tip, moving left and right of the joint in all directions to give strength to the intersection. *Do not* build up the solder; let it smoothly taper off for a flush effect. Carefully turn the panel over by sliding it over the worktable edge, tipping it down to the edge of the table helps to support it, while you hold the bottom and a side edge. Lift the panel on to the edge of the table, move further back on the table and evenly lower the panel toward you, down to the tabletop. Repeat the abovementioned same steps to the back of the panel.

While working with the lead came you probably noticed, the came does not hold the glass snugly under the flanges and when turned, the glass rattles within the came framework. This occurs because glass can vary in thickness while the height of the heart remains consistent. Special heights can be obtained but the average came is made to accommodate 1/8" thick glass with room to spare. To make a came (lead or other type) glass window weatherproof, glazing cement is forced under the flange and down beside the heart to fully cushion the glass within the came.

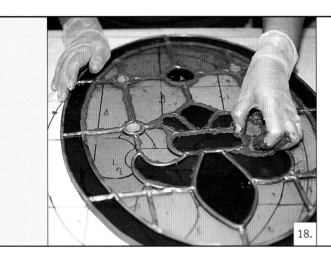

18.

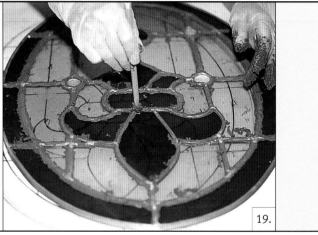

19.

This can be the messiest part of the stained glass craft, but it is one of the pivotal final steps to finishing the panel. Produced in a variety of colors, glazing cement comes in black, neutral white, bronze and gold. If the glass is transparent and you are using came that will ultimately be black or a dark color, select black. If the came has been treated with a nickel plate, choose white. Brass came will be enhanced with gold cement. This matters because you will see a tiny bit of the hardened cement under the flanges; if you do not clean the glass properly residue will show in the corners.

18. Wear gloves if possible as the glazing cement has a thick, oily, putty-like consistency that is difficult to clean from your fingers. Form the cement into a small round ball. With thumb and forefinger push it under the flange in one area until no more can be added. Move to where the cement flowed out from under the flange and force cement under that area. Work your way around each piece of glass in this fashion until the entire side is done. Turn the panel over again and repeat the process on the reverse side. The second side should not require as much, since the first side pushed the glass down on the came flanges. The application on the second side forces the glass to be centered in the came with cement on either side.

21. Use a soft stiff bristled brush to scrub and push the powder into the sides of the lead came coating the cement, causing it to thicken further. This action will also clean the glass and came, as the powder is slightly abrasive, and will remove the flux and cement oils from the surface of the panel. The lead came will begin to darken eventually to a black satin sheen as it is brushed and the lead joints will shine. Brush the now gray whiting off to one side for use on the reverse. Turn the panel over again and remove the extra cement, adding used and new whiting and brush until clean. On transparent glass, brushing it will require several passes since small spots of cement will appear on the opposite side you are cleaning. Tip the balance of the gray whiting to the waste bin and clean the bench.

19. Now, take a pencil or pointed stick and trace completely around the came to remove the excess cement. Recommend this be balled up and returned to the container for future use.

20. Wear a dust mask as you sprinkle whiting on the panel in the center area.

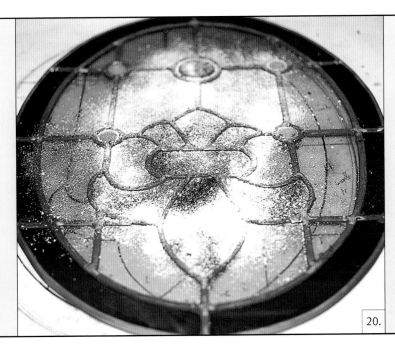

20.

21.

22.

23.

24.

**Fleur de Lys**
Pat Daley,
Kaleidoscope Stained Glass,
Sarasota, FL

22. This panel was made for an oval frame and the out side lead "**H**" came flanges need to be trimmed to allow the panel to be seated in the rabbet in the back. Mark where the panel does not fit.

23. Using the nippers, cut the flanges until the panel has clearance into the rabbet.

24. Use a wood block to lightly tap around the outside came to firmly seat the glass. Add glazing points or silicone the panel to hold in the frame. Commercial brass mountings are available to affix to the frame for hanging with a decorative chain.

LEFT
**Crystal Cross**
Calvin Sloan,
Star Bevel Studio
Riverview, FL

Beveled glass and lead
came method in a flowing
circular design.

LEFT
**Victorian-style panel**
Calvin Sloan,
Star Bevel Studio
Riverview, FL

This piece combines
textured glass, a bevel
cluster and faceted jewels.

RIGHT
**Trees**
Angela Rozic,
Sarasota, FL

Three mirror panels fill the
space between four 1930s
style leaded trees.

ABOVE
**Quatrefoil**
Pat Daley,
Kaleidoscope Stained Glass,
Sarasota, FL

Oval panel using antique
and "seedy" cathedrals with
a *spun rondel center* built
with lead came.

Commissioned by Richard
Gagne, Sarasota, FL

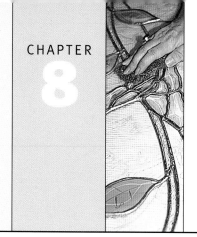

CHAPTER

8

BUTTERFLY SIDELIGHT

# THE copper FOIL method

The copper foil method is the wrapping of a cut and ground piece of glass with an adhesive backed copper strip in preparation to join the pieces with solder. The copper is heat conductive and allows the lead solder to flow onto it coating the copper with a raised bead of lead to simulate lead came. The space between pieces of glass is filled with lead to create a "heart" as found with came and gives strength to the project. There is no putty process as the foil is pressed directly onto the surface of the glass.

There is some question surrounding the claim that this technique originated in the Tiffany Studios for use in the windows and delicate lampshades. Many people have erroneously credited any stained glass lamp-shade assembled with lead came or copper foil as a "Tiffany." A Tiffany-style shade is made on a mold using the copper foil. In truth, no one knows exactly who developed the concept to use thin strips of sheet copper, wrapped and folded the edges on the glass, spot solder the seam closed, and then, solder the pieces together—but the Tiffany Studios' use of the technique in building shaped lamp shades made it famous. The foil technique had come in favor with the

evolution of copper foil. Instead of tedious strip-cutting now, there is adhesive backed foil in a variety of sizes and multi-color backings. Two weights are available: 1.5 mil and 1 mil thickness. I prefer the thicker 1.5 mil for its strength in forming, folding and burnishing to the glass. When selecting foil for glass, your choices are copper and black and silver backing. If you are using cathedral, antiques or bevels, the color of your patina will influence what foil you use.

A. Black or silver backed foil should be used with transparent glass resulting in black or copper patina. This will make the inside of the glass edge invisible under the solder line.

B. Opalescent glass will require a plain copper back, as the extra effect of silver or black will not be visible, regardless of patina.

C. Avoid using black back foil on white or on light colored opalescent because it will give a black halo effect around the edge of the glass and create a flaw in your project, as light will expose the dark shadowed edge.

The width of the foil is important, as most glass is 1/8" thick. The popular sizes are 3/16", 7/32" and 1/4". There is 5/32" for extra thinness and 5/8" to 1/2" and 1" for more coverage. The glass has to be centered in the foil to show the same amount on each side when folded over to provide proper support. Two foiled pieces, side by side, will show you how wide your solder line will be. Mouth blown antiques and new antiques are thinner than 1/8", so the 3/16" foil appears to have the same amount one side as 7/32" would have on standard 1/8" thick glass. If you wanted to create a wider solder line on antique, use the 7/32" or 1/4" for more coverage over the edge of the glass. The advantage of foil is it can be combined in different widths on the same piece to vary the solder lines. A wider application of foil can also be cut with a razor or x-acto blade to give wavy, jagged or extreme motion to one side or both sides in shaping the solder line. In conjunction with decorative solder techniques, you can create scales, pearl drops, hammered and many other effects on the solder line. In the following photo examples, another favorite technique of Tiffany is used: laminating two glasses together for color effect as well as the copper foil method.

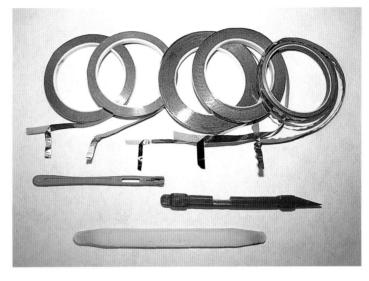

Supplies for Copper Foiling:
1. Foils – copper, silver, black and wave
2. Hand foilers
3. Burnishing fid

This copper foil project is a sidelight (the long narrow window next to a front entry door) designed for a customer in Sarasota, Florida. The condominium rules prohibit removing the existing single pane of glass. The location of the sidelight is under an extended roofline forming a canopied walkway. The sun does not shine direct light but in the afternoon bright light will enter between the closely set buildings. Privacy is not an issue as the existing glass has a slight, large rough pattern but that concern has to be considered in selecting glass that addresses specific needs beyond its art value. The accepted design was beveled butterflies flitting around an ascending, curvy vine with green beveled leaves. The customer wanted clear glass in order to maximize natural light along with highlight colors of green and pale champagne to match the floor tiles and carpets. The beveled butterflies were only available in clear so the solution was to cut a matching back piece of color to attach to the bevels.

This laminating process was used by the Louis Tiffany Studios and others to create subtle shadings with semi-transparent opalescent glass in varying combinations of two or more glasses, cut to exact shape, placed together in lead or foil and soldered in place. The protruding glass would be installed to the outside and be unnoticed from the inside. In this application, the raised butterflies will be two glasses thick (bevel and champagne color), as well as on the inside (face) of the sidelight.

1. Carefully trace the bevels on the colored sheet and cut the pieces.

2. Grind to the line.

3. Dry and place under the bevel to check fit. Mark for any adjustments for further grinding.

4. Choose a copper foil that will not show around the edges of the glass and will be wide enough to overlap both sides—in this situation, I chose copper backed 3/8" wide. Firmly hold the two pieces together, center the glass on the foil, and wrap it around the two pieces on the edges (a bevel has a tapered edge and will not be as thick as two 1/8" pieces foiled together).

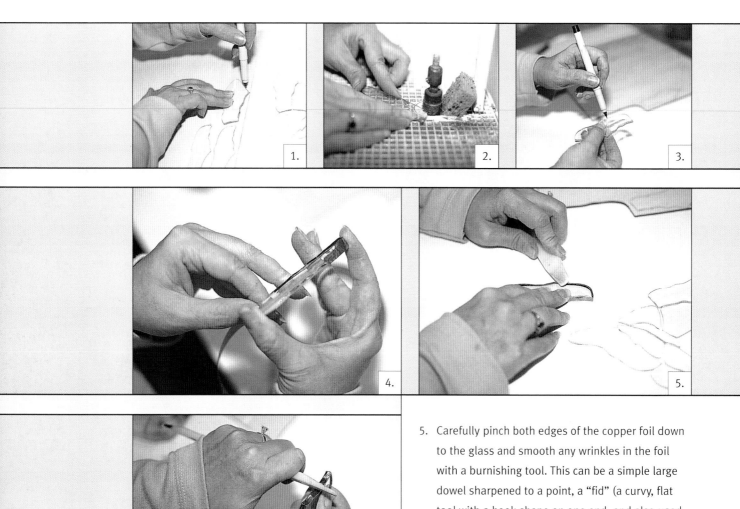

5. Carefully pinch both edges of the copper foil down to the glass and smooth any wrinkles in the foil with a burnishing tool. This can be a simple large dowel sharpened to a point, a "fid" (a curvy, flat tool with a hook shape on one end, and also used with the lead came method), or a wide flat "book-binder's bone".

6. Gently rub the foil down on the face and edges of the glass pieces, forcing the adhesive to stick to the glass making it resistant to the flux. Otherwise, the flux would destroy the adhesive, flow under the foil and weaken the project. In addition, too much rubbing will stress the foil by making it wavy and the adhesive will not stick to the glass. Two or three strokes will be adequate.

7. After the bevels and champagne colored glass have been foiled, they were arranged to complete the butterfly. Spot solder holds the pieces together, and then, a more complete solder line is produced on one side only.

8. The paper pattern is laid on the bench and 1" x 1½" x 5' strips of wood are positioned and secured to gain a straight edge to place the glass against. Allowance was made for the 3/8" wide brass **U**-channel, and at the 1/8" depth, the glass panel will sit in the **U**-channel when framed on the drawn pattern. The side guides of wood and straight edge are secured on the line indicating the 1/8" inside the **U**-channel. This will guarantee a straight and square panel built to fit within the

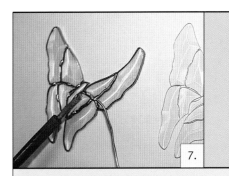

7.

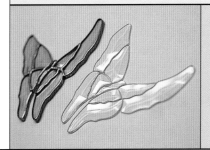

In the photograph, notice the difference in edge thickness from the bevel cluster on the right to the completed champagne butterfly on the left.

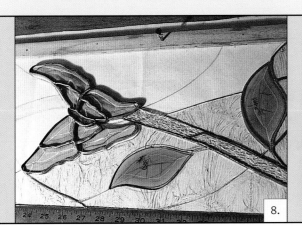

8.

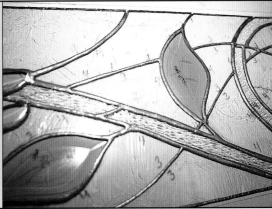

This completed section shows how the changes in foil width create varying solder lines — 1/4" thick vine sides contrast to the thinner 1/32" lines.

existing sidelight frame. A champagne butterfly, one of the beveled green leaves and cut pieces of textured clear are laid in position on the paper. These will be marked with numbers indicating the size of the silver backed copper foil that will be used to wrap the individual glass pieces.

In this project, the ice-textured vine needed outlining with a heavy line, but the leaves and background glue chip glass needed to be thinner. The bottom of the butterfly wings swirled downward in a spiral effect and needed to taper from the wide line (due to thickness) to a finer point before going off at the edge of the panel.

This was accomplished by changing the foil's width on a piece, and the adjoining glass. In the photo, the cut and ground glass was laid in position and marked with a "4" for 1/4" and "3" for 7/32" foils. Straight lines on the edge indicated where to begin and stop that foil sizing: the crystal side by side, 1/4" and 1/4" yields a wide line; a combination of 1/4" and 7/32" narrows the solder, and 7/32" only, side by side, results in a thin line. At the top of the vine where it circled back in on itself, the foil was trimmed on both sides of the glass pieces to a finish as thin as possible. When the panel is foiled and soldered, the next step is to frame it with the brass **U**-channel.

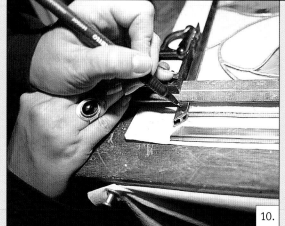

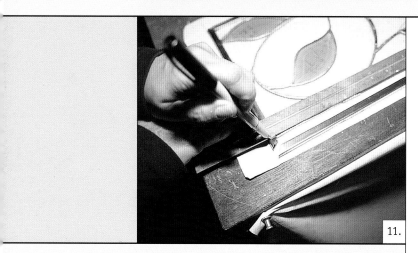

9. Using a chop saw with a fine tooth metal blade and adjustable miter bed, cut a 45° angle at the end of a 6 foot brass **U**-channel. The same result can be achieved with a wooden miter box and a hacksaw with a fine tooth blade. One tool company is producing a small fixed miter box and saw designed for hand-cutting zinc and brass came and channel. It may now be available at your local supplier.

10. I have matched a long sidepiece and a short top piece with mitered corners on one corner of the top of the sidelight, on the far side and deliberately cut the top piece longer than needed to allow room for measuring the cut. Marking the brass to allow the glass to be seated 1/8" inside depth and be at the 45° corner, takes patience using a ruler. Place the channel so it is seated on the glass edge in position. Since the channel is overall 3/8" wide, measure from the edge of the **U**-opening 1/8" in towards the center of the brass and mark it with a "dot" in the area of brass that extends beyond the glass. This defines where the shelf inside the brass is located. I will mark another dot, using the same method, at a spot where the brass is fitting over the glass panel. A straight line will visually show the shelf inside, with the glass seated on the shelf.

11. Using a combination square, align the ruler portion on top of the glass panel and to the edge. Mark the brass **U**-channel with a straight line continuing to the edge of the glass. This will show the location of the corner edge of the glass on the shelf when the brass is cut to size. The result will be a "crosshair" marked on the brass.

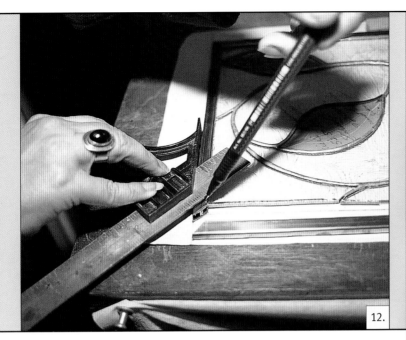

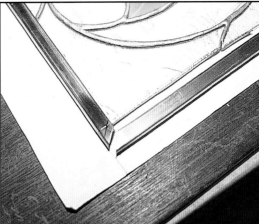

The marks now should look like this.

12.

13.

12. Place the edge of the square to position the ruler at a 45° angle through the "crosshair" marks on the brass. (See Figure 8.1)

13. After the 45° angle is cut and the brass **U**-channel is placed onto the glass in position, note the corner of the glass is exactly at the edge of the shelf, inside the open cut. Also, in the photo, see the pattern line showing the outside edge of the **U**-channel. When the long piece is fit into position, it will sit exactly on the line and come up to the solder line at the leaf.

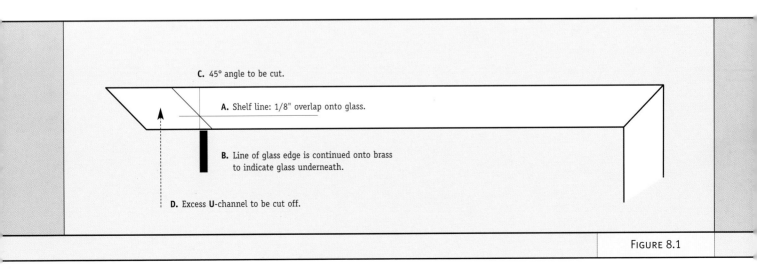

**C.** 45° angle to be cut.

**A.** Shelf line: 1/8" overlap onto glass.

**B.** Line of glass edge is continued onto brass to indicate glass underneath.

**D.** Excess **U**-channel to be cut off.

FIGURE 8.1

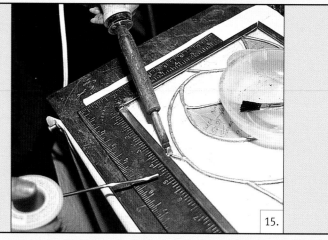

14. To guarantee a square fit and to help hold the channel for soldering, use a carpenter's square to ensure a snug fit on all four corners. Then, place a wide amount of solder left and right to make a solid joint but no wider than the tip of the iron.

15. After the corners are finished go down the edge, pre-heat the brass next to the copper foil and allow solder to flow onto the foil and a small amount — approximately 1/8" — onto the brass edge. Caution here to avoid overdoing the solder on the brass, as it can't be removed. Blend the new solder into the existing solder line by reheating into the cold solder as needed.

Carefully turn the panel over by sliding it to the edge of the table and raising the side upwards, move it evenly backwards to rest on the table. Check and see if support is needed under the glass panel as the panel is slightly raised on the laminated butterflies. Continue soldering all the copper foil, attach the brass **U**-channel to the solder lines and solder the corner miters.

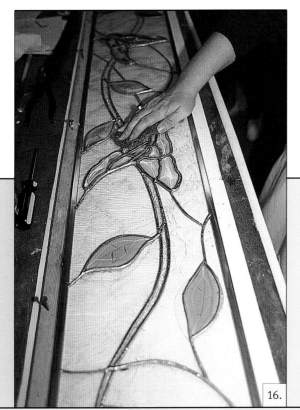

16. If you let a project sit too long after soldering, it will be necessary to clean the solder lines by rubbing them with #000 steel wool to remove any oxidation. Moreover, a light wipe with wet sponge, dish soap and water will clean the glass and flux residue from the panel in preparation for patina.

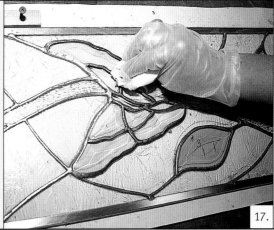

16.

17.

17. Wear a protective glove and use a slightly damp paper towel to apply the patina to the solder lines. The patina used on the sidelight was copper although two other colors were available: black or antique brass. Patina will only affect the lead solder and not the brass **U**-channel. If zinc **U**-channel had been used it would require a special patina for zinc, only available in black or copper. Patina is best described as a chemical electro-plating that will inhibit lead oxidation and give a warm color to the solder lines when cleaned and polished. After the patina is applied to one side, wash and dry the panel—turn it over—repeat the patina process and clean.

The finished panel was delivered and installed. The customer had planned on quarter round wood trim to frame it but liked the look of the brass so the trim piece was not added to the secured panel.

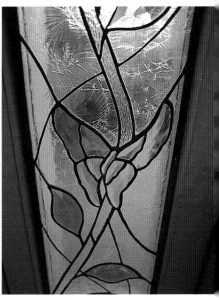

**Butterfly Sidelight**
Pat Daley,
Kaleidoscope Stained Glass,
Sarasota, FL
Commissioned by Bernice
Handelman, Sarasota, FL.

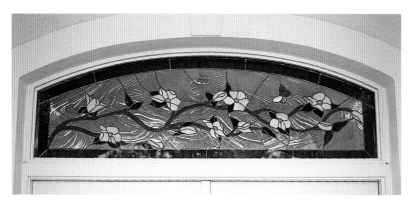

**Floral Panel,**
Calvin Sloan,
Star Bevel Studio,
Riverview, FL

Use of color, and clear bevels
to create intricate mirrored
floral pattern with fracture
and streamers as background.

ABOVE

**Magnolia Blossom
(interior and
exterior views),**

Pat Daley,
Kaleidoscope Stained
Glass, Sarasota, FL

Transom with
Spectrum's iridescent
clear Baroque glass
and opalescent branch
and flowers with
butterfly and grape
Waterglass border.

From the inside the
border color shows
and the grain layout in
the white opalescent
blossoms.

Commissioned by
Mr. & Mrs. Christian
Christensen, Venice, FL

LEFT

**Beveled Glass Entrance,**
Calvin Sloan,
Star Bevel Studio,
Riverview, FL

Example of large cut bevels
in a traditional door, side-
lights and transom.

**Hummingbird and Flower**

Designed to be a frame within a frame. The oval centerpiece flows into the outer diagonal frame with the bird and flower edges. "Flashed glass" has been sandblasted away for the bird head and wings.

BELOW

**Vine & Flowers Sidelight**
Pat Daley,
Kaleidoscope Stained Glass,
Sarasota, FL

Privacy sidelight using textured English Muffle glass.

Commissioned by Shirley Brodsky, Sarasota, FL

ABOVE

**Blue Heron,**
Bob Williams,
Queen Valley, AZ
Arched window insert in master bath. Courtesy of Marilyn Moman, Queen Valley, AZ.

LEFT

**Sails at Sunset**
Harold Wyman,
Bradenton, FL
Abstract piece.

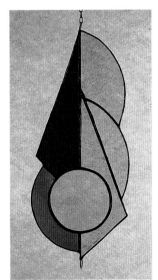

# BUILDING a DIMENSIONAL OBJECT

Stained glass in forms other than lamps and windows may intimidate a person. To handle a glass box knowing that it could break if improperly held can make anybody nervous. But then again, everyone uses a drinking glass without a second thought other than how far to fill it and to place it on a flat surface. The glass box is stronger than a fragile, thin walled drinking glass because it is made with 1/8" glass and solder. A glass box would survive a fall from a table with a crack or two whereas a drinking glass would be shattered. Therefore, a stained glass box is not the delicate object it appears to be. Since you have learned how to score and break glass, you now know how strong glass actually is and can approach building a dimensional object with confidence.

The box in this chapter uses the technique of plating in making the lid. A customer who wished to give a wedding gift, agreed to the suggestion of a useful stained glass box with the invitation preserved under glass in the lid. Since there was a mix of color on the invitation, Spectrum #307s, smooth, iridescent pearl white was chosen to complement the printed card. The iridescent highlights on the glass accented the colors in the floral pattern and the overall white background was suitable for a wedding gift.

**Keepsake Box**
Pat Daley,
Kaleidoscope Stained Glass,
Sarasota, FL

Commissioned by Patricia
Mallard, Sarasota, FL.

## Box Size and Drawing on Glass

The first step in making a box is to determine the over-all size, height and width. The box size in this commission is preset by the size of the invitation, a 6" square. The depth of the box sides is usually $1\frac{1}{2}$" to $2\frac{1}{2}$", on all four sides but that does doesn't have to be the case. This box will display an object in the top so a "raised back" is preferred to present the object for viewing. In the photograph, there is a drawing of the box body, high in the back and sloping to the front to aid in visualizing the overall shape. The box body is $1\frac{5}{8}$" high in the back tapering to $1\frac{1}{4}$" to the front. The whole box can be cut from a 6" x 12" piece of glass.

Measurements made directly on the glass were labeled for cutting making it easy to position for soldering. Since the box is to have a finished square top of 6" x 6", a line was drawn in from the straight edge of the glass to be cut 6" wide. You must allow for the thickness of the glass and reduce the width of the pieces to $5\frac{3}{4}$" ($\frac{1}{8}$" each side = $\frac{1}{4}$") to allow the lid to fit flush to the outside of the box. Draw a line $\frac{1}{4}$" in from the edge and extend it from the bottom up exactly 6". This is a working area for measuring the box sides and the 6" x 6" remaining piece is the lid.

The first measurement for the height of the box was made across the back of the box, $1\frac{5}{8}$" in from the edge of the glass and side-to-side, $5\frac{3}{4}$" across. This is marked "the back of the box" where the hinge will be placed. The second measurement will be the right side of the box and needs to have a taper to tilt the lid downward to the front of the box. Start measuring on the line just drawn, $1\frac{5}{8}$" up on the right side and $1\frac{1}{4}$" up on the left side, and draw another line connecting the two. This is labeled "right side"—$1\frac{5}{8}$" back corner joins to right side edge of the $1\frac{5}{8}$" x $5\frac{3}{4}$" piece, the back, and $1\frac{1}{4}$" joins to the front $1\frac{1}{4}$" x $5\frac{3}{4}$" piece.

Measure up another $1\frac{5}{8}$" from the right end of the line just drawn and mark it. Measure the distance from the bottom edge of glass and on the left, from the bottom edge of the glass, mark the same measurement on the left side so the two marks are even – then draw the line. This should be $4\frac{7}{8}$" (3 times $1\frac{5}{8}$") up from the bottom edge of the glass, and $5\frac{3}{4}$" across. On the left side, on the new line, mark the front measure downward $1\frac{1}{4}$" and draw the line across and down to the top mark for right side—the $1\frac{5}{8}$" opposite back corner. This is the left side of the box and should be labeled as so.

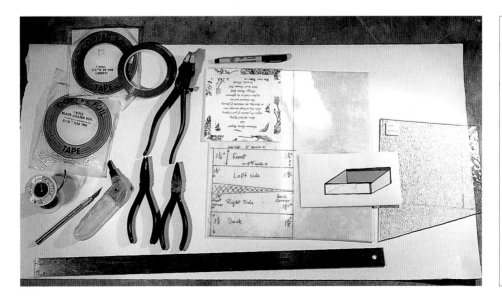

Project Supplies:
1. Copper foil
2. 50/50 solder
3. X-acto knife
4. Glass cutter
5. Runners
6. Breaker/ groziers
7. Ultra-fine pen
8. 12" x 12" Spectrum 307s iridescent glass
9. 8" x 6" Spectrum 100GG clear glass
10. Box body
11. Drawing
12. Cork-back ruler

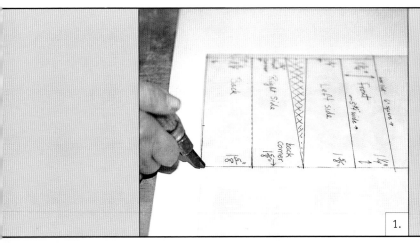

3.

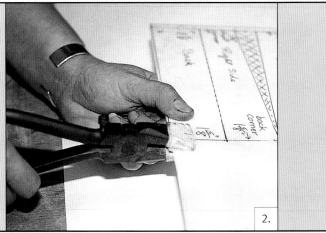

2.

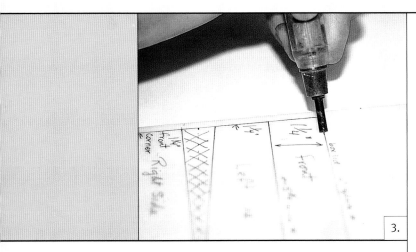

1.

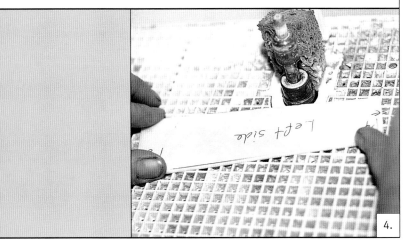

4.

In the photograph, the space between the tapering lines has been filled in to show what is waste glass. The front is the last piece to draw. It's dimensions are $1\frac{1}{4}$" up from the straight line of the left side on both sides, and drawn $5\frac{3}{4}$" straight across. The remaining glass will be used for the box lid.

1. When cutting a piece of glass larger than 6" x 12", cut the long line to remove the strip on all marked sides of the box. Cut the 6" x 6" box lid area off, and set it aside.

2. Score and break off the 1/4" strip beside the pieces marked for the box.

3. Then make all scores for the box pieces and break them apart using the runners.

4. Lightly grind all sides on the four pieces to accept the foil and wipe clean, keeping the marks on the glass.

5.  The back piece that receives the hinge requires special foiling to support the hinge and lid. Using 1/4" copper-back, begin to foil by "lipping" about 1/8" on the top 5³/₄" side, and down the 1⁵/₈" short side, across the bottom 5³/₄", up the 1⁵/₈" short side ending about 1/8" on the top 5³/₄" side.

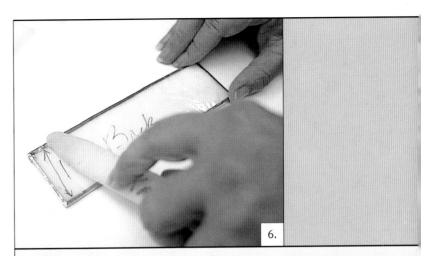

6.

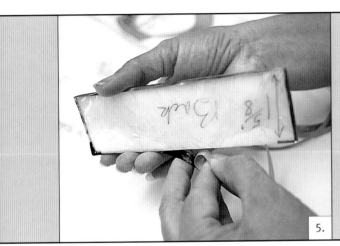

5.

7.

6.  Fold down to the face of the glass and lightly burnish the foil. The second size of foil to apply is 5/16" across the non-foiled top edge. This extra width foil will support the weight of the raised box lid by having more foil secured to the glass face inside and outside of the box. Burnish the foil down.

7.  Trim any overlapping 5/16" foil down the short sides to match the 1/4" underneath. Foil the remaining 3 glass box sides with 1/4" foil.

**Star & Diamonds Box**,
Pat Daley,
Kaleidoscope Stained Glass,
Sarasota, FL

Kiln shaped amber glass provides a fire-polished open edge for this cathedral and opalescent round box.

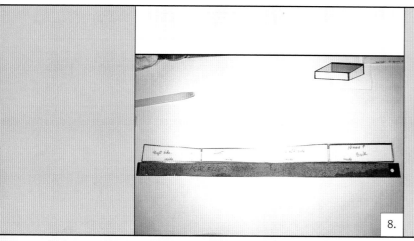

8.

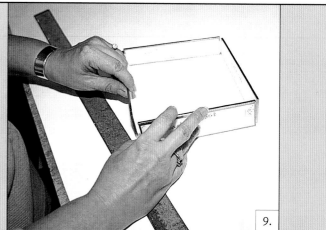

9.

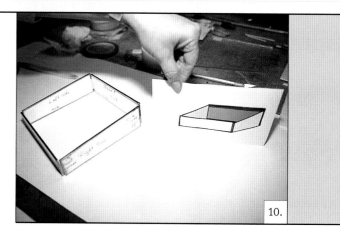

10.

## How to Make a Square Box Square in Two Steps

8. To assemble the pieces of glass, lay them face down so you are looking at what will be the interior of the box. From left to right across a straight edge, position the pieces clockwise on the box body starting with the right side piece. The high $1^5/_8$" back corner is placed farthest to the left on the end of the straight edge. The second piece is the $1^1/_4$" x $5^3/_4$" front piece matching the low right side. The third, the left side matches the $1^1/_4$" short side to the front piece, and finally, the high, back piece measuring $1^5/_8$" x $5^3/_4$". Be sure to place the back piece with the wide hinge foil to the top. Secure the short sides tightly together with strong masking tape and be sure the glass is flush against the straight edge when it is taped.

9. Lift the 4 joined pieces by the top edges, and raise the entire piece toward you, standing it up. Fold the sides in toward you into the shape of a 6" square with the iridescent surface facing outward and the white, to the interior.

10. Now you should have a "body" in the desired shape with sloping sides that match the drawing.

**Green Agate Box**,
Harold Wyman,
Bradenton, FL

Incorporating natural material in stained glass, the agate dictated the shape of the box body.

11. Use 50/50 solder because it solidifies quicker than 60/40 on all dimensional objects. Heat the soldering iron and flux the corners (see Figure 9.1) of the box. The masking tape has held the corners in position but in order to be in correctly positioned after fluxing, pinch the edges of the glass together as in the diagram below and spot solder the top that joins the glass edges together on all four corners. Carefully turn the body upside down and repeat the same steps for the bottom of the box. This will secure the sides for the next step—filling the corners with solder.

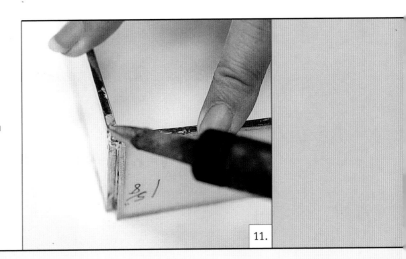

11.

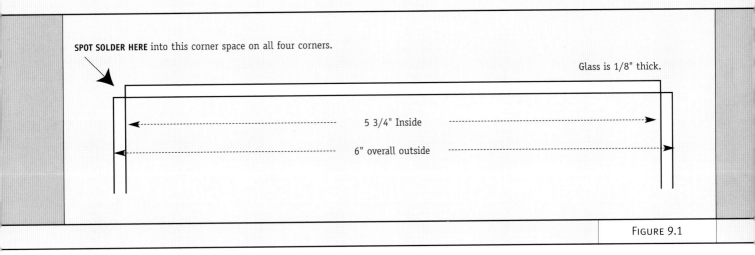

**SPOT SOLDER HERE** into this corner space on all four corners.

Glass is 1/8" thick.

5 3/4" Inside

6" overall outside

FIGURE 9.1

12. Begin to fill in the corner space by coating the copper foil with solder, slowly adding additional solder. If you have any uneven fitting corners, the masking tape will help prevent the solder from melting through the gap.

13. Turn the box to rest on the corner on the table, remove the masking tape and solder the inside of that corner to a finished line. Repeat these same steps for each of the other 3 corners.

14. This process "firms the body" into the 6" square but remains flexible until the outside corners are completely filled. To do this, slowly add more solder to the outside corner spaces until they are filled and rounded with a finished bead line.

12.

13.

14.

## Attaching the Bottom of the Box

The next step is attaching the bottom of the box. A textured clear glass, (Spectrum 100GG—clear crystal ice) is placed on the table. Position the box body on the bottom glass so that the edge of the bottom is flush with the face of the sides as in Figure 9.2.

If one side is even with the bottom glass, trace around the outside of the remaining 3 sides. If the texture distorts the line underneath, turn the textured clear glass over and use a ruler to draw straight lines to guide the cut. Score and break on these lines and lightly grind so the bottom is even on all sides. Gently round the sharp corners to fit under the rounded box corners.

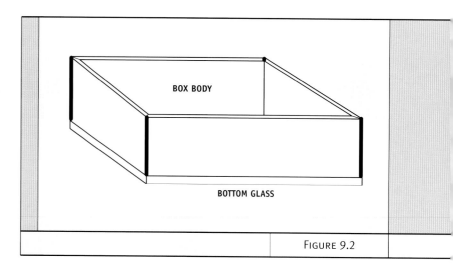

BOX BODY

BOTTOM GLASS

FIGURE 9.2

15. Since the body of the box rests on the glass, extra foil must be added to the face of the bottom piece of glass to accept solder. Quarter inch copper foil is laid on the face next to the edge and burnished in position on the textured side. The body glass is 1/8" thick and will cover half of this foil, leaving 1/8" inside for solder.

16. The next step is to wrap the bottom glass with 1/4" foil and burnish as usual in preparation for soldering.

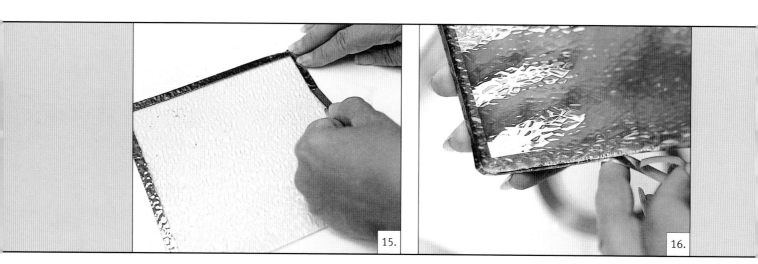

15.

16.

17. Center the box on the glass (be sure the wide hinge foil on the back panel is not on the bottom), brush flux inside at the base of the side and to the exposed foil on the face of the bottom glass. Then, spot solder to secure the sides to the bottom. Start again with a finish solder bead around the inside of the box bottom.

18. When this is completed, turn the box on the side and solder the bottom glass to the box sides.

19. Upon cooling, turn the box body upside down and apply a solder bead to the foil on the bottom glass.

**Laminated & framed wedding invitation**
Pat Daley,
Kaleidoscope Stained Glass,
Sarasota, FL

Commissioned by Janette Collins, Sarasota, FL.

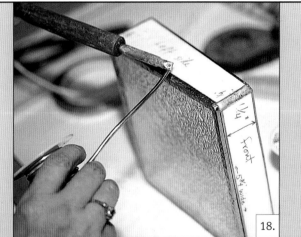

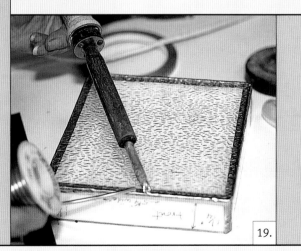

## Applying the Edge Roll
## Finish to Box Lip

At this point, the box body is together with the bottom attached and soldered. The lip of the box has not been soldered and is addressed next. The process involves applying an "edge bead" or "edge roll". A proper edge roll will withstand touch and occasional cleaning without snagging or tearing foil from the glass. Too often, in rushing to complete a piece, this important finishing procedure is overlooked. Copper foil that is not burnished on the glass will not resist flux or water and be weakened. Heat from too small an amount of solder will slightly lift the foil, exposing a sharp metal edge capable of cutting skin. Therefore, it is very important that all glass edges have a reasonable amount of solder to prevent an accident.

17. Stand the box on a side and flux the foil facing up, on the top and inside the bottom lip.

18. Add solder to the face of the foil from one corner to the next. If a small amount drops and solidifies over the edge on the top do not remove it, continue along. Apply the same to the bottom inside lip. If it overflows on to edge of the glass, it is to be used in the next step.

19. Now, rotate the box so that all four outside and inside faces are treated in the same manner and resemble a photograph.

The purpose of adding solder to the edge is to build a rounded "C" shape over the foil as shown in Figure 9.3. Place the box flat on the table. You have applied the solder to the inside and outside of the box with extra drops now on the top edge.

20. The extra solder drops will be melted by using only the round corner of the iron tip, and will flow evenly on the rim of the box lip, left and right. Extra solder, beyond the foil's capacity to hold, will fall away down the sides of the glass. You want to melt the solder so it forms the round C shape so you don't see the square edges of the glass underneath.

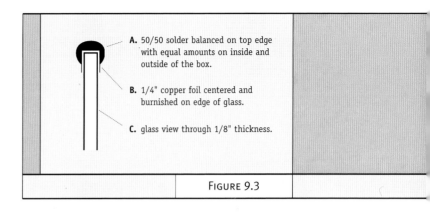

**A.** 50/50 solder balanced on top edge with equal amounts on inside and outside of the box.

**B.** 1/4" copper foil centered and burnished on edge of glass.

**C.** glass view through 1/8" thickness.

FIGURE 9.3

21. If you have a space on the rim without solder, add a small amount to the tip of the iron and place it where it will melt, joining to the solder around it. Support the box as you solder down the tapered side. The melting solder needs to be kept level to flow evenly on the sides and top rim. The hinge foil will require additional solder as it is wider on the inside and outside in order to support the hinge and lid. It will take practice to achieve a uniform round edge roll. Your patience will be rewarded by going slowly, using only the round corner of the tip of iron to control the heat and flow of the solder.

20.

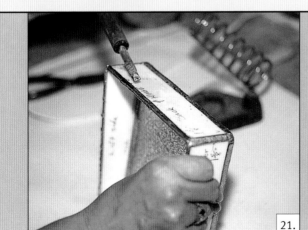

21.

This is the finished edge rolled box. As you can see the result is worthwhile.

## Making the Box Lid

This lid will be in two pieces—the top is clear, the bottom is the iridescent white, and sandwiched between the glasses will be the wedding invitation.

21. Take the 6" x 6" piece that was placed aside and trace it on a clear, single strength piece of glass.

22. Cut the clear glass and lightly grind the edges. Lightly grind the 6" x 6" piece at this time, clean and dry both pieces.

23. To sandwich any flat object such as pressed flowers or paper it is necessary to secure it to the base glass, the iridescent glass in this case. Use a touch of clear drying glue to the back of the object and position it on the base glass. Position the paper in the center of the base glass, press on the corners to glue it down and let dry.

24. Clean the clear glass top on both sides and check to remove lint, dust or fingerprints. Handle this glass by the edges and lower it onto the base glass with the dried (glue) invitation in place.

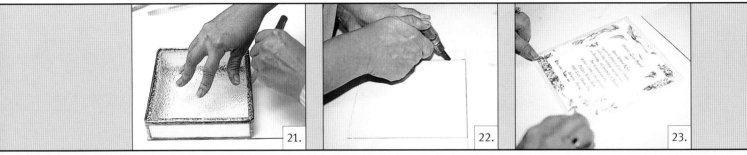

25. Firmly hold the two glasses tightly and evenly together, and begin wrapping with 3/8" wide foil. Once you have gone half way around on 2 sides, it becomes easier to hold and finish the second two sides. Two additional layers of foil are applied to extend the foil onto the face of the glass and back of the glass. This step helps to seal the glasses from flux seepage and is done according to the method in Figure 9.4.

After the foil has been folded down and burnished, you need to wrap the face and back of the glass once around with 3/8" foil next to the edge, where the hinge will be installed. This step provides extra soldered area support for the hinge.

25.

Here is the finished foiled lid with the extra foil applied.

26.

26. Lightly flux and apply solder for an edge roll around all lid sides and edge. There is more surface to build the 50/50 solder on, so this should be easier to do than on the box body. When you have completed this stage, use only a damp cloth sprayed with glass cleaner to wipe the flux residue from the finished lid. Do not hold the lid under running water or in water. Even though you have double foiled the edges, there is no guarantee the work is water-proof. Clean, thoroughly dry and place it aside.

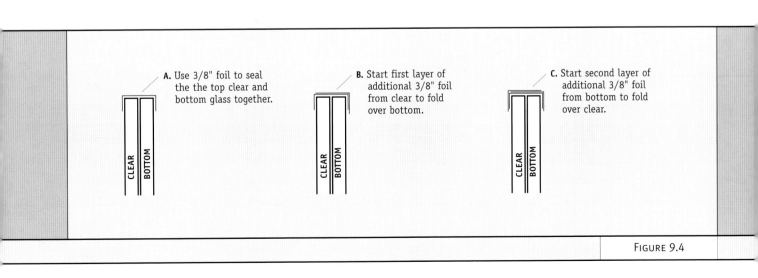

**A.** Use 3/8" foil to seal the the top clear and bottom glass together.

**B.** Start first layer of additional 3/8" foil from clear to fold over bottom.

**C.** Start second layer of additional 3/8" foil from bottom to fold over clear.

CLEAR BOTTOM

CLEAR BOTTOM

CLEAR BOTTOM

FIGURE 9.4

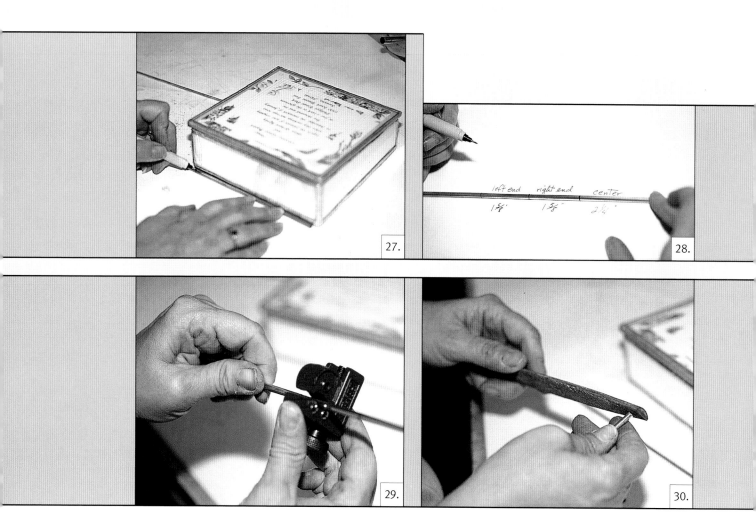

## Making the Hinge

27. Measure across the back of the box body where the extra foil was added for the hinge. This should be about 6" wide. Measure between the soldered corners that should be about 5 1/2". To make the hinge you will need a 5/32" diameter rod to fit inside a 1/8" tube. Copper or brass are acceptable as they will solder and can be purchased at your local glass supplier or hobby shop in 12" lengths. Place the tube at the base of the box to the back and mark a piece 5" long. This will be the overall size of the hinge extending across the back of the box.

28. The hinge tube will be divided into 3 pieces called "knuckles." Two smaller knuckles will be attached to the body at either end and a larger center knuckle will be soldered to the lid. Measure and mark the tube for 2 pieces, 1 5/8" long and the remaining piece will be 2 1/4" long as shown in the photograph.

29. You can cut the tube with a hacksaw or use a mini pipe cutter.

30. After cutting the tube into the three knuckles, file any burrs off the open ends so the rod will pass effortlessly through the tubes.

Lay the three knuckles in a line and place the rod next to them. Mark the rod for cutting about a 1/4" shorter than the tube so the rod will be slightly recessed inside the hinge. Cut the rod with a hacksaw or miter saw. File both ends to ease insertion into the tubes. In this sequence, slide the tubes onto the rod: first, the short 1 5/8", next, the middle 2 1/4", and last, a short 1 5/8".

## Soldering the Hinge to the Box

31. Place the lid on top of the box body. Pick it up, and stand the lid and body together on the front of the box. This will make the lid flush with the front on the tabletop. You will have to move the lid side to side to position it evenly on the box body. When you have it in position, secure the lid to the body with an elastic band, holding them together.

32. Then place the hinge in "the valley" between the lid and body where you have applied the extra foil on the back. You can slip paper between the end knuckle and the lid preventing solder attaching to the lid. Flux sparingly only the end knuckle next to the box body. Solder will flow where flux is, but you want to keep it away from the lid. Initially, you want to spot tack both end knuckles to the box body with solder.

33. Then gently add small amounts of solder until the knuckles are firmly soldered to the body. The center knuckle is soldered to the lid on the face edge of the lid, so place a paper between the tube and body of the box to prevent solder flow. Sparingly flux the center tube to the lid adding small amounts of solder until it is firmly attached with some build up to the lid. Remove the elastic bands, paper and wipe the hinge area clean.

34. In a measured tone say "open sesame", and the box will open. A small oval chain is added to stop the lid from opening too wide by attaching it 3" from a front corner to a side of the edge roll on the lid. By trial and error, you will find "the sweet spot" where the lid balances on the back of the box. You accomplish this by stretching and attaching the opposite end of the chain inside the bottom of the box, in the solder seam, near the front corner. Now the box is ready to fill with memories.

31.

32.

33.

34.

# separate elements become one

This charming kitchen clock uses a simple technique of overlaying finished components on a flat base and attaching them with either solder or clear silicone adhesive. Also demonstrated is how to drill a hole using a diamond bit on the glass grinder.

The background for the clock face is a 10" square white opalescent. The size was determined by the availability of printed brass clock faces that are either 5" or 7" in diameter. Since this is to be placed in a larger room and would be referred to often, I selected the 7" face. The face will be centered in the square and still have enough border to place a grape cluster, butterfly and vine with leaves on it.

**Kitchen Wall Clock**
Pat Daley,
Kaleidoscope Stained Glass,
Sarasota, FL

1. A five-piece butterfly was cut from yellow opalescent glass and a small piece of brown. The 1/4" foil has an edge roll applied on all pieces and the upper and lower portion of the wings are soldered together.

2. The butterfly has the wings raised slightly upwards from a brown body and are soldered to the body, while the outside wing edge is resting one side on the burnishing fid.

3. The butterfly has soldered pearl eyes added to the head on the edge of the roll. Copper wire antennae will be added and the butterfly cleaned, rinsed and patina applied before final placement on the clock frame.

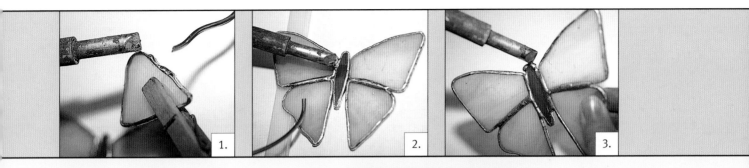

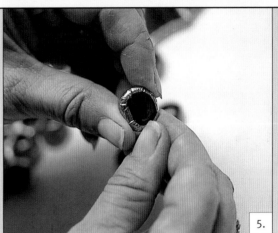

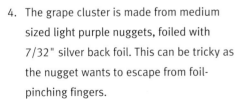

4.  The grape cluster is made from medium sized light purple nuggets, foiled with 7/32" silver back foil. This can be tricky as the nugget wants to escape from foil-pinching fingers.

5.  A solution is to very lightly grind around the nugget giving it a rough texture to adhere the foil and begin folding the foil over on the bottom of the nugget.

6.  Any uneven foil overlap is trimmed with a knife before burnishing the front and bottom of each nugget.

7. An edge roll is applied to nuggets that will be on the outer edge of the cluster and this can be done easily by holding them with a wooden "spring type" clothespin. This keeps the flux, hot glass and iron tip off your fingers. Rotate the nugget around until the solder is lightly coating the rim of the nugget.

8. Arrange the nuggets in a pleasing fashion (as grapes do not grow in straight sided clusters, make lopsided or uneven edges for a natural shape) and flux. Melt the solder on the iron tip and drop in a random fashion on the nuggets spot-tacking them together. Then continue to fill the spaces by randomly moving around the glass cluster. You do this to allow some of the heat from the solder to dissipate to avoid cracking the nuggets by working one area too long. The pattern for the grape leaves is placed under the cluster and marked for cutting. The grape leaves are added to the cluster and the entire cluster is cleaned, rinsed and the patina is now added.

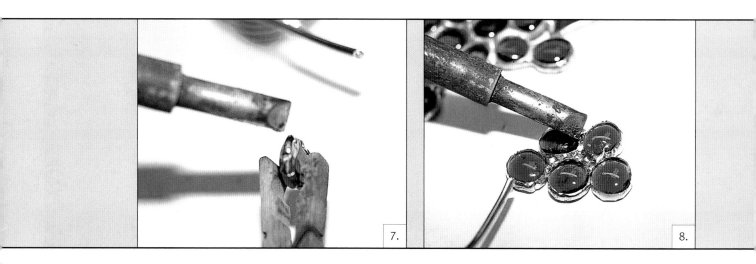

7.

8.

9.

9. Now the grape cluster and the butterfly are finished and placed aside for the moment. The clock background glass has to be drilled in the center to insert the spindle of the clock movement. This is the point where the movement is secured to the clock face and hung on the wall. Since the clock is 10" square and the numbered face is 7", there will be a border of $1^1/_2$" on the sides. Center the round face and outline the hole in the center and the outer shape. The standard hole size is 1/4". You will need to mount a diamond 1/4" bit on the shaft of grinder.

10. At the grinder, turn the glass upside down so you are able to see the center mark. Slowly lower it so the inside of the circle touches the edge of the bit first. Be aware that the spin of the bit can cause you to slip the glass across the bit until there is an indentation to seat the bit. Then with slight pressure you can pull the glass down onto the spinning bit at a 45° angle.

11. Remove it after a minute to drip water into the groove to clean the slurry and lubricate the bit. Reseat the glass in the same groove and work the pressure downward pivoting around in a circle centered on the bit.

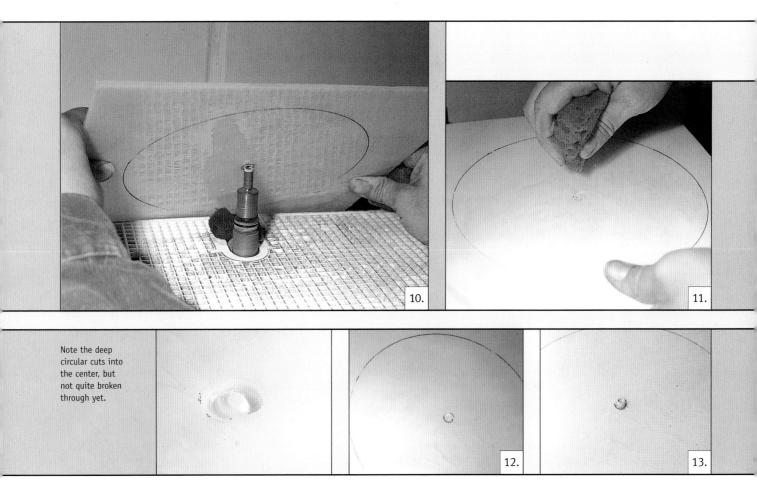

Note the deep circular cuts into the center, but not quite broken through yet.

12. To avoid plunging through from underneath and chipping the edge, turn the glass over and find the center from underneath—you can almost see through the light spot because the glass is thin.

13. Again, slowly lower the glass onto the center at the 45° angle and in a moment, you should have grinding slurry beginning to show on the surface in the deep hole. The 1/4" bit is moved around inside the hole rounding it as needed.

14.

15.

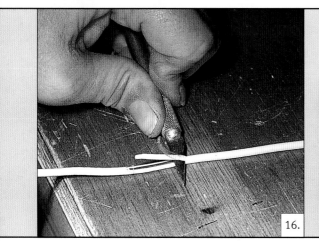

16.

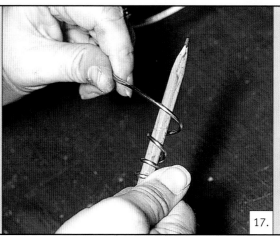

17.

14. At this point, check it against
the metal clock face for fit.

15. The raw edge of the white back
ground glass is covered with a
3/8" copper **U**-channel and all
corners soldered front and back.

16. Three strands of copper 14-gauge wire are needed to make the twisted grape vine, two leaf stems and one curled tendril. Cut a length of coated electrical house wire and insert a knife blade sideways into the plastic sheath. Hold the knife firmly and pull the wire towards you to strip a portion of the plastic upward all the way to the end of the wire, removing the plastic sheath.

17. Loosely wrap the bare wire around a pencil to form a spiral, letting it get larger at the end.

18. Position it behind the grape cluster leaves and mark where to cut.

19. Solder it into a seam on the back of the leaves. This will protrude above the back as a curled grape tendril.

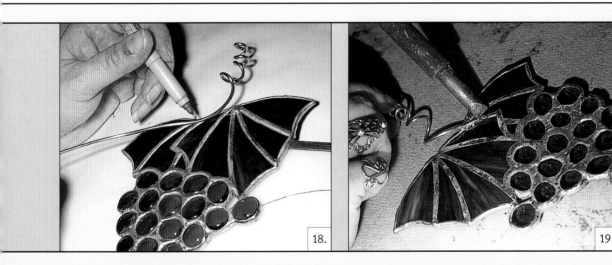

20. Now arrange the grape cluster and butterfly on the clock face and note that there is space for two smaller leaves cut from sheet copper.

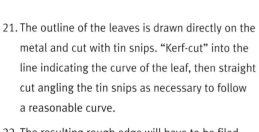

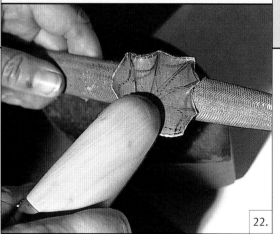

21. The outline of the leaves is drawn directly on the metal and cut with tin snips. "Kerf-cut" into the line indicating the curve of the leaf, then straight cut angling the tin snips as necessary to follow a reasonable curve.

22. The resulting rough edge will have to be filed and sharp edges blunted. The leaf can be textured using a straight cutter's tapping ball struck with the ball peen face of the hammer on an upturned flat iron or anvil. This will add a "cupping" dimension to the leaf that is be rippled using pliers to bend, forward and backward, along the veining lines from the center of the leaf.

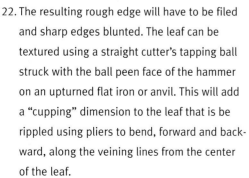

23. The wire to make the vine is about 16" long folded in half forming two 8" strands. A single strand of 8" wire is cut with one end soldered into the "V" shape to create 3 strands. Heat strands with the iron and tin coat with solder do not have to exhibit an even coating—the copper wire can show through in spots.

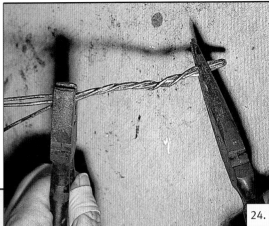

24.

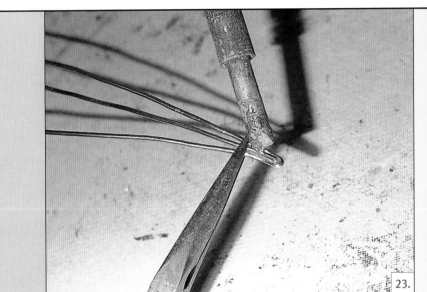

23.

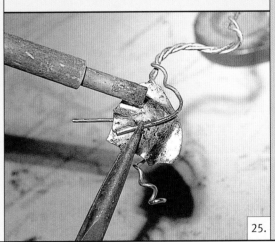

25.

24. For an uneven, natural twining vine effect, grasp the soldered end with pliers and turn the wires together with difference degrees of tightness as you progress down the length of the copper strands. Leave three strands untwisted about 3" back from the end and curl one as a small tight tendril.

25. Hold a copper leaf with pliers and apply heat with the iron. Flux and tin coat the entire leaf with solder. You can add solder to one single strand to fully "tin it", and attach the back of the leaf to it. Do this also to the second strand and remaining leaf. Now it's time to clean, rinse and patina the completed vine as a separate element.

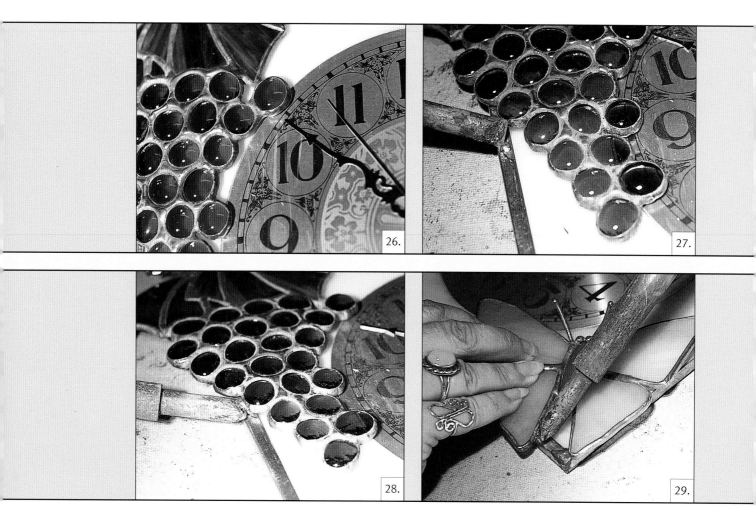

26. When making a clock, it is very important to note that any object applied on the brass face of the clock must allow the 3 hands to move around the numbers without touching anything. The grape cluster is very close to this limit on placement. Mark the edge of the copper **U**-channel where the grapes touch for soldering.

27. It is easier to heat and add a spot of solder where the grapes will be applied, than to try and heat the **U**-channel and the edge roll together on the grapes.

28. Once the spot of solder is on the **U**-channel, position the grapes' rolled edge over it and melt solder to solder, spot-tacking the cluster on. Bend and shape the twisted vine and leaves into a pleasing shape and solder into position on the top of the **U**-channel anchoring behind the grape cluster, and spot on the **U**-channel, as needed.

29. Finally, do the same to the butterfly in the lower corner. You can use a cotton swab or twisted paper towel to apply patina to the newly soldered spots and wipe clean with a damp cloth.

30. Clean the outline from the edge of the clock's brass
face from the glass and remove the protective coating from the face.

31. Position the face over the drilled hole and insert
the clockwork's spindle through from underneath.
There will be a thin rubber washer and a brass nut
to thread on the spindle forming the clock front and
holding the clock's motor work to the glass. The
spindle shaft has two shaped areas to accept the
hands, one round and the other oblong. Fit these
in sequence, per the clockwork instructions. The
second sweep hand is screwed into the opening
on the end of the spindle shaft.

Since the clock itself may be heavier on the right
side because of the grape cluster, you may need to
turn the motor works on the back to position the
hanging loop at an angle to hold the clock level on
the wall. Add the battery... set the time and enjoy
your new clock!

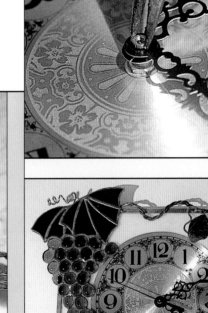

31.

30.

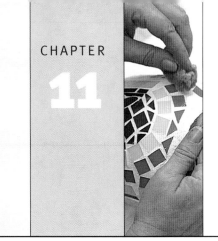

# MOSAICS AND GLASS

Mosaic work is an outgrowth of inlay techniques using multicolored glass, tile, marble or other stones glued or cemented on a base to decorate furniture, walls and floors. This style of decoration originates as far back as 3500 BC based upon furniture found in excavations at Ur. The best known surviving ancient works are at Pompeii and across the Mediterranean region including religious decorations in old Byzantine and Roman churches up through the 14th century. Mosaics fell out of favor during the Renaissance period and have only recently enjoyed a revival in the middle 19th century through simple floor and wainscoting tile designs primarily in public places. Now within the past few years there is a renewed interest in mosaics using stained glass as face material in cast cement garden stones applied to wall mounted fountains, bird baths, decorative garden benches and tables, and even fused, hand made glass tiles for interior functional and decorative home use. Since there are a large number of stepping

stone patterns and instructions (actually any glass pattern can be used to create a mosaic as long as it fits within the wide variety of molds or on the chosen flat base material), I will not repeat here what can be easily accessed through a variety of sources. However, I will go one step beyond what everyone else is doing and focus on a dimensional mosaic vase.

**Mosaic Vase**
Pat Daley,
Kaleidoscope Stained Glass,
Sarasota, FL

Stained glass scraps can be your source for mosaic glass as there are two types of styles. The planned design and utterly random shapes, with a little cutting and fitting, will find their way into pleasing design works. The method for this project is a planned design using four, 5-piece tulip and leaves, placed within four yellow arches and backfilled with a sky blue color. The balance of the vase will be another shade of blue and filled white grout.

1. A medium size clear glass vase is the base on which to apply the glass tiles. Any craft supply shop will have these vases in the floral section. Select one with smooth sides.

2. Take a wide piece of masking tape and fold it in half—sticky side in. This will become the measuring tape for the widest part of the vase.

3. Wrap the tape around the widest part of the vase and mark where it meets on both left and right ends of the tape.

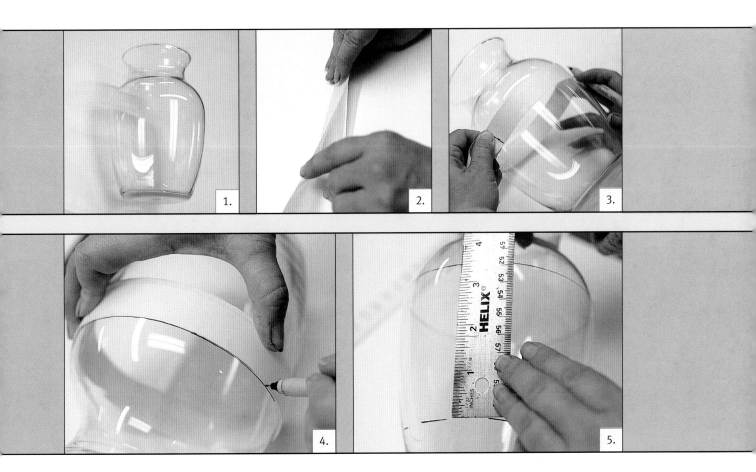

4. Draw a line around the vase using the top of the masking tape as a straight edge to indicate the height limit of the tulips.

5. Measure down from the line to mark the bottom of the design on the vase, about $3^1/_2$".

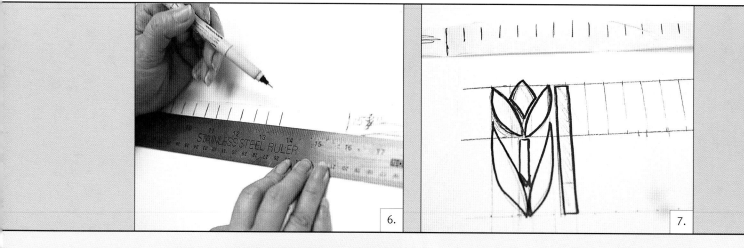

6.

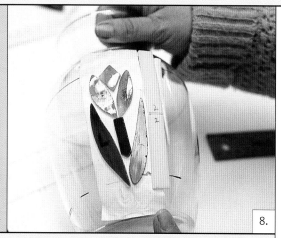

7.

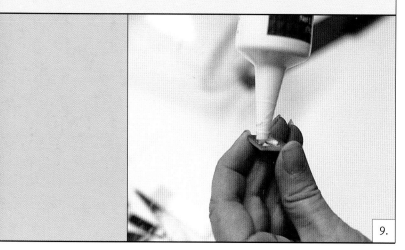

8.

9.

6. Lay the masking tape flat on the table, measure the space between the marks into 1/2" squares. The tape measured the vase at 15$^3/_4$" in diameter. Draw the same measured lines on a piece of paper to create 1/2" wide spaces, 3$^1/_2$" tall and 15$^3/_4$" long. This is the grid you use in which to fit the elements of your design.

7. Draw your design slightly smaller with spaces between the pieces to allow for the grout lines. The long straight pieces may be slightly angled as on a tulip's leaves, but there is the possibility that the glass will protrude from the side of the vase, requiring it to be filled with grout.

8. Once the central elements, the tulip and leaves are cut and ground, tape them together as they would be on the vase and place them on it. This will expose any glass that will not fit as close as possible to the contour of the vase, and may need to be repositioned or replaced.

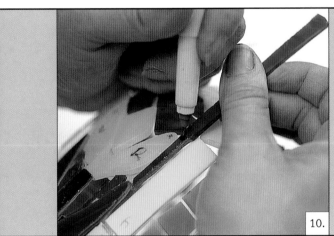

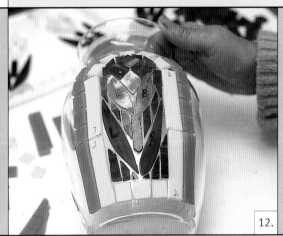

9.  If everything is satisfactory, remove the pieces from the tape and use clear silicone adhesive to glue the pieces on the vase within the drawn lines to position. In this design, four tulips will be glued in each quarter of the vase. Spread the glue evenly on each piece of glass and place on the vase. You may have to balance the vase, keeping it level, so the glass does not slip until the glue can set.

10. Now that the arch is in place around the tulip, cut long narrow strips of the background glass. Place each strip of glass in the space and mark for cutting.

11. For narrower strips, grind the sides of the glass strip to fit a given area before you cut it off from the long strip. Remember, mosaics need space for grout, so fit the glass to be at least 1/16" away from an adjoining piece.

12. When all the glass has been placed on the vase, let it sit overnight to allow the glue to fully cure.

13.

14.

15.

13. Use a smooth grout if you want a flat texture fill. If you want to use a colored grout, select one that will be a complementary accent to the glass colors. For this project, I used smooth white tile grout. Mix to the consistency of a heavy cream by slowly adding water to the powder and stirring. Let the grout slake for 10 minutes—no stirring.

14. Wear protective gloves while working with grout, as it will contain a small amount of Portland cement that has a skin irritant. Fill the spaces between the glasses with grout, but remember the glass has sharp edges.

15. Once the grout is applied, smooth it by finger-tip until it is even with the surface of the glass. Select a height on the neck of the vase to establish a grout line, and do the same on the bottom edge on the side of the vase.

16. As the grout begins to dry, carefully wipe off the excess from the face of the glass with a dry cloth or paper towel. After the excess grout is removed, let it dry overnight.

17. The next step is to seal the grout to protect lighter colors and waterproof it. Apply the tile grout sealant with a sponge or small brush to all the grout lines and let dry. This step completes the mosaic vase.

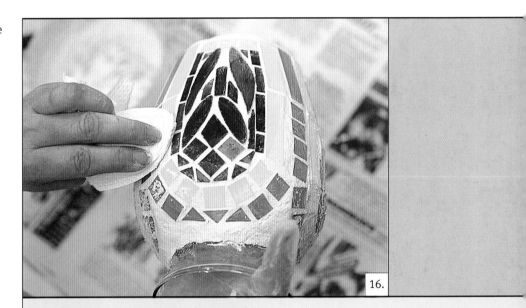

16.

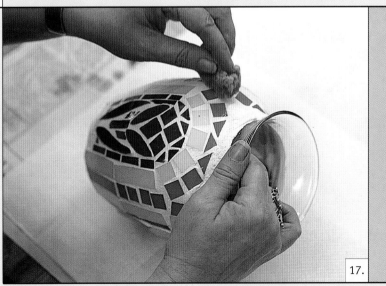

17.

LEFT
**Mosaic Vase**
Pat Daley,
Kaleidoscope Stained Glass,
Sarasota, FL

ABOVE
**Two Parrots**
Michelle Alexus,
Nokomis, FL

The pattern, made
for this mosaic
garden stone, came
from a photograph
of two parrots.

LEFT
**Eye of Horus**
Pat Daley,
Kaleidoscope Stained Glass,
Sarasota, FL

Mosaic garden stone
based on the design
of an Egyptian bracelet
belonging to Pharaoh
Sheshonk II, Dynasty 22.

RIGHT
**Sunburst**
Brum Studios,
Sarasota, FL

Mosaic stone.

ABOVE
**Tropical Fish**
Brum Studios,
Sarasota, FL

Mosaic stone.

BELOW
**Sunny Cool**
Brum Studios,
Sarasota, FL

Mosaic stone.

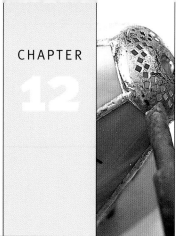

# BUILDING
## BETWEEN THE LINES

Lampshade is the next word that immediately comes to mind when stained glass is mentioned. Decorative windows were permanently installed in residences, became passive items—taken for granted—and remained when the property was sold. Conversely, stained glass lighting was the only portable form of stained glass. Dining room lamps and table lamps were often handed down through the family or sold, even destroyed as fashions changed.

Lampshades are active, compared to the passive window, as we use them on a continuous basis for general or mood lighting. The original, glass lampshades of the early 20th century were lit by low wattage bulbs and cast soft light into the room. The current high wattage bulbs cast a much brighter light and generate higher heat temperatures for lampshades. Accordingly, antique lamps are lit with lower watt bulbs to retain the true, intended appearance by the craftsmen as well as to protect the shade's metal construction from the bulb's heat.

There are several points to consider when deciding on your lampshade. First, is *purpose*—do you want it to provide accent light or room/task lighting? This criteria, will dictate the size of the shade. A suitable size for a dining room or kitchen table should be at least

12" in diameter to disperse light to the edges of the table. Uninterrupted light will travel in a shape matching the profile of the shade, downward from under the shade, and depending on its height from the tabletop will influence the radius of the light. Billiard game table stained glass lights are rectangular-shaped to illuminate the corner pockets, round or square tables

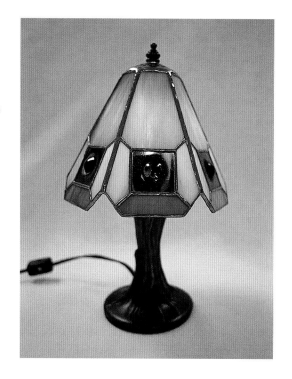

for card playing or dining will usually have round or large, square shapes to cast light evenly on the table top. Small accent lighting using a shade 6" to 8" in diameter will give small areas of light directly around the lamp base but not much beyond, again depending on the height of the base. The density of the glass mutes the light transmitted through the sides of a glass shade, unless it is beveled or cathedral type glass.

Second point is to consider: *the choice of glass.* Any shade made of cathedral, antique or wispy/translucent glass will show the electrical components and white-hot light bulb. This glass will work for a hanging lampshade with a multi-arm candelabra and clear flame bulbs that are intended to be seen. However, it is not a good fit for a table lamp with the harp, socket and single bulb glaring on the top of the lamp base. The usual choice is an opaque or opalescent glass that hides the hardware and avoids the hot spot created by the bulb. Transparent or bevel accents may be used in an area of the shade that does not directly face into the bulb. If cathedral glass is to be used, consider a heavy textured glass that breaks up the glare of the bulb and conceals the hardware.

Another choice is the actual shape of the shade, although this is somewhat determined by the use of the light. The basic shade consists of a combination of three sections: crown, body and skirt.

ABOVE
**Tiffany-style Lamps**
Pat Daley,
Kaleidoscope Stained Glass,
Sarasota, FL
Commercially produced.

LEFT
**Grape Trellis**
Harold & Shirley Wyman,
Bradenton, FL
Based on an original Tiffany design from a pattern in "Lamp Works".

OPPOSITE
**Six-panel Lamp**
Pat Daley,
Kaleidoscope Stained Glass,
Sarasota, FL

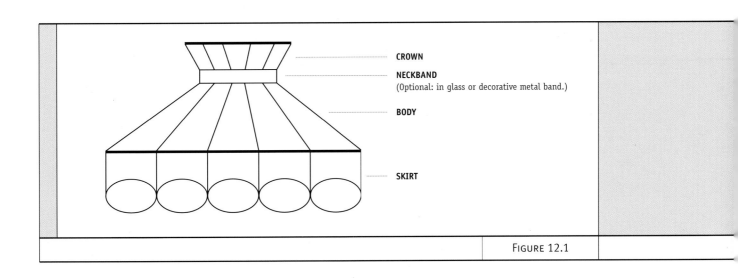

CROWN

NECKBAND
(Optional: in glass or decorative metal band.)

BODY

SKIRT

FIGURE 12.1

## Lamp Hardware

The hardware used to assemble a shade for hanging or mounting on a lamp base is as follows:

**Spider:** made of brass or steel, has 3 or 4 "arms" radiating from a thick center ring and is used to attach the electrical components to the shade. The spider is centered inside at the top of the body at the narrowest opening (below the neckband and crown) and soldered to the inside seams of the body. The arms can be slightly bent to fit the sides of the tapered glass. For best results, pre-tin the arms with solder before applying to the solder seams and carefully secure solder to the shade.

**Threaded Nipple & Rod:** is a brass hollow tube 5/8" in diameter with threads on the exterior, smooth inside. Comes in various short lengths and threaded rod lengths that can be cut with a hacksaw, if needed.

**Locknuts & Washers:** are brass hexagon nuts and washers used on either side of the spider's ring to secure the threaded rod or nipple.

**Porcelain Socket with Metal Cap:** Porcelain is mandatory to hold a light bulb in reverse position, as it is heat resistant. *Standard brass sockets have a cardboard liner that will dry out, slip down on the hot bulb and can char or even catch fire.* Porcelain sockets have a cap that covers the lamp wires attached with 2 screws, and has a receiving opening for the threaded nipple and a locking screw to secure it. This is positioned at the end of the threaded nipple or rod and at the appropriate level in the shade to allow the light bulb to be centered in the body.

**Cast Loops:** come in a variety of loop sizes and finishes, bright or antique brass or nickel. These can be tinned to accept patina to match the finish of the shade, as desired.

**Chain:** Lengths of chain are usually available in 3' segments. Recommended link gauge (the thickness of the wire used to make the link) is 10 or 8 gauge— the lower the number, the thicker the link. For best results, use chain spreaders to open and close links. If you do not have this tool, grasp the link with two pliers at the split and twist one end to the side. Do not pull the link open as it will be difficult to close to match the opposite end, however, twisting it back is easier to align the ends to close the opening.

**Lamp & Ground Wire:** comes in a variety of color— white, black, brown, clear, silver, copper and gold. It is best to match it with the chain color to help conceal it against the links. Always purchase more than you think you need, as it is easier to cut excess off than to make another trip to the hardware store.

**Wire Nuts & Electrical Tape:** The stranded lamp wire will be twisted around the solid, heavier gauge house wire and covered with a plastic wire nut cap. The electrical tape, wound around the cap and onto the joined wires, will secure the connection while hanging the shade. Never let the shade hang from only the two wires, as it will pull the connection apart and fall. Be sure to match the number of wires and gauge to the proper size wire nuts—ask for sales assistance if you are not sure.

**Cross Bar:** The cross bar is a wide flat steel strip with slots on either side of a threaded center hole that is attached to the electrical wire box in the ceiling. This screws at both ends to pre-drilled holes in the box. A short piece of threaded nipple is added to the center hole to feed the lamp wire through, and to attach the canopy cover and loop. The slots are used for the canopy screws to secure the cover to the bar.

**Ceiling Canopy:** is a large decorative cover with loop that will conceal the electrical wiring in the ceiling and will hold the chain and lamp.

The following describes the parts of a lamp base and hardware for mounting a shade:

**Spider:** 3 or 4 way for shade top openings larger than a 3" diameter. This can be used under a high domed or shaped vase cap to support the shade if there is no crown or it is used alone with a crown.

**Vase Cap:** a flat or slightly cone or dome shape brass disc with a hole in center. This is used if a crown is not added to the lamp body. The cap fits to the top of the shade and is soldered to the seams on the outside and securely soldered around the inside of the shade, to the body. A variety of shapes and sizes are available such as square, pentagon, hexagon, octagon, or round shaped. The preferred caps are pierced with holes to allow the heat from the light bulbs to escape. There are several types of heavy cast brass caps available and Tiffany reproduction styles that involve matching neck rings, spider-like wheels and vase caps.

**Finial:** decorative knob that is threaded on the small stem on top of the harp and protrudes through the vase cap. This secures the shade to the harp.

**Harp:** Elongated U shaped heavy wire that holds the shade over the light bulb. A flat platform with a small stem supports and secures the shade to the harp with a finial.

**Saddle:** the small platform under the socket that has two upright arms to receive the harp's bottom ends. The two loose caps on the harp fit down over the arms to secure the harp to the saddle.

Examples of lampshade bases.

**Lamp Base:** this can be any pleasing item: a ceramic vase, wood, or metal or glass object capable of being wired as a lamp and able to hold a shade, glass or other top for a lamp base.

**Threaded Rod:** a piece of hollow tube with exterior threading lining the interior of some lamp bases to pass wire through the saddle and attaching the socket for wiring. In some instances, a threaded nipple is used if the channel for the lamp wire is very open as inside cast metal bases.

**Bushing:** a round plastic plug inserted in metal bases to pass and protect the lamp wire from roughcast edges of the hole. It allows the lamp wire to protrude from the base back when the base is a flat bottom rather than pedestal style.

**Shade Riser:** a solid small cylinder with a threaded hole inside and threaded stem on top. This goes on the harp stem when the shade needs to be raised in 1/2" or 1" increments to fit the base. The finial would attach on the stem as it would on the harp itself.

One question that is always asked—"How do I know what size lamp base will go with my shade?" There is no hard and fast answer. The lampshade and base have to be in reasonable proportion. A shade too small will look awkward perched on the base. A shade too large will cover more of the lamp base, and worse, if too wide, increases the chance of tipping over. Lamp bases are usually measured from the bottom up to under the saddle. The harp size is usually stamped on the top or under the platform at the finial. Harp sizes are varied and can be interchanged. If a harp is somewhat short, a shade riser may be necessary. The basic, rule of thumb is, place the shade on the base and see where the edge falls. If it is even with the saddle and allows room for a hand to reach in and under to turn the light on or off, the height is correct. If the shade is slightly lower than the saddle but the lamp wire has an inline off/on switch installed, a shade riser may not be needed.

The diameter of the shade in relation to the bottom of the base is not as obvious. One suggested measurement is the lamp base be two thirds of the bottom diameter of the shade. A 6" wide panel lamp will look and be stable on a base at least $3^1/_2$" across the

bottom since if the centered shade were divided in half, only $1^1/_4$" would be extending beyond the base. Often it becomes a matter of judgment, depending on the style of the lamp base.

In that regard, a simple lampshade would look out of place on an ornately decorated base, as the reverse would also be true. A multi-piece shade with various colors and design would overwhelm an understated, minimalist base. Try the shade on several bases once the height is known and step back to look. It becomes a matter of personal preference and you know where you will place the lamp in relation to your home's decor. In the end, it's up to you to find the balance with the shade style and base.

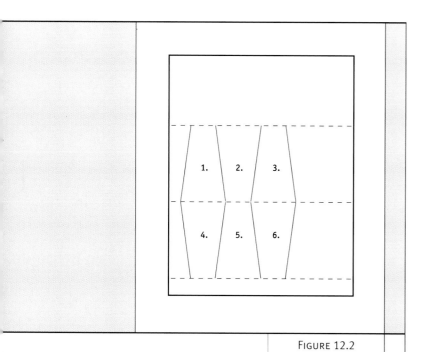

Figure 12.2

## A Six Panel Lamp

Building a panel lamp as a small accent table light is straightforward as long as you follow these guidelines.

Keep the design in proportion to the panel to be made. Don't overload the panel with many small pieces as they become hard to handle, remember you have to make at least 4 of each. Choose colors that will compliment each other and the area intended to be illuminated. Most important of all, build a framing jig and grind to fit the pieces within the frame for consistent and easy assembly.

The accent light made for this chapter has 6 panels and uses 6 antique pressed square jewels as a highlight. The glass colors were chosen to be in a Southwestern or Florida environment—teal jewels, teal and white opalescent for the main colors of the body with pink coral highlights left and right of the jewels.

The pattern was cut from a heavy paper and laid on top of the sheet for tracing. When working with straight-line edges, they can be shared for cutting when positioning the pattern on the glass. This procedure saves cutting time and glass usage. By cutting the two rows of glass, it is assured the panels will be the same height and relatively easy to run the score to break the individual panels from each other.

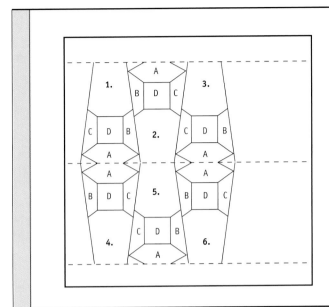

**SEQUENCE FOR CUTTING OUT AND
RETRACING ALL PIECES (do to all panels)**

**A =** Bottom teal/white piece

**B =** Coral side piece on right

**C =** Coral side piece on left

**D =** Straight line drawn connecting B & C at top to
indicate square jewel and larger teal/white top piece

FIGURE 12.3

1. Trace the design as one complete panel at a time
   on the glass. Then, each of the segments are cut
   out and re-traced, one at a time, to show the cut
   lines within the panel.

2. Make a jig using straightedge guides to follow the
   shape of the outside of the panel and grind to fit
   each piece within the sides. Foil the individual
   pieces with 3/16" or 7/32" foil and replace into the
   jig for soldering. Solder the front of the panel and
   remove from jig. Solder the back of the panel and
   set aside to assemble the next remaining panels.

When the individual panel is soldered front and
back, clean both sides with a damp cloth and dry.
Use 7/32" foil to wrap the two sides and top of
the panel. Apply the wider 1/4" foil to the bottom
panel edge. Apply the solder bead edge roll
remembering to trim any foil overlap up the sides
on the 7/32". Build up the solder bead only on
the bottom edges of all the panels at this time
and damp clean carefully to avoid disturbing the
unsoldered foil on the sides.

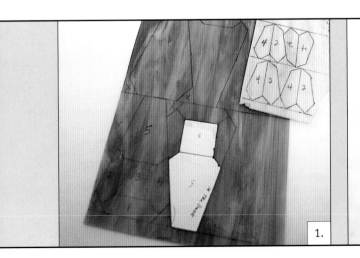

1.

2.

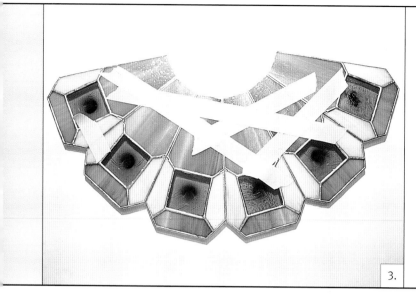

3.

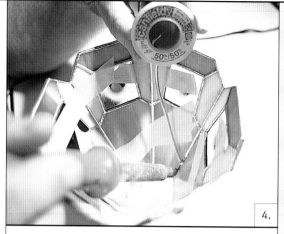

4.

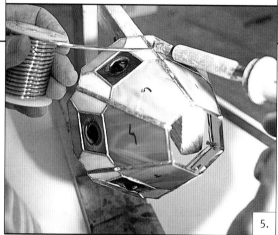

5.

3. Lay the completed panels in a fan shape face up to arrange in order for assembly. Check for color matching or any variation in size so the corners of each panel match the next one. Turn them face down to the table so the backs of the panels are presented in the same fan shape. Use masking tape to join the panels to one another across the copper seams.

The proper position for the panels for soldering is not overlapping at any point but one edge to the next edge as shown. Fill the seams with solder to stabilize the panels, then, fill to level with the glass.

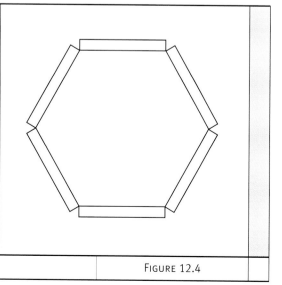

FIGURE 12.4

4. There are two ways of bringing the panels into shape for soldering. The first is to carefully lift the taped panels from underneath and place them (narrow end) into a round container, such as a bowl. This will force the panels into a round shape and support the sides while spot soldering the seams to firm the panels. Be sure your container will be resist melting as the hot solder will roll down into the center of the inverted cone and drip into the center of the container.

5. The second way is to slide the taped panels onto a firm board and cover with another firm board as a sandwich and turn over. Remove the board. The face of the panels is now presented with the tape underneath. Grasp the narrow part of the panels and lift off the board. The panels will automatically fold up into the cone shape of the shade. Tape the open side closed, and begin to flux and solder the top seams.

Prop the shade on a side and level the seam to be soldered. A simple cross beam can be assembled using an upright piece of wood secured to a wide base with a wood arm extended at a right angle and held in position with a "C" screw-type clamp to the upright wood. This will allow the shade to be placed on the arm and leveled for finish outside soldering. A raised solder bead is required down the length of each seam. This gives strength to the shade but it is still slightly flexible.

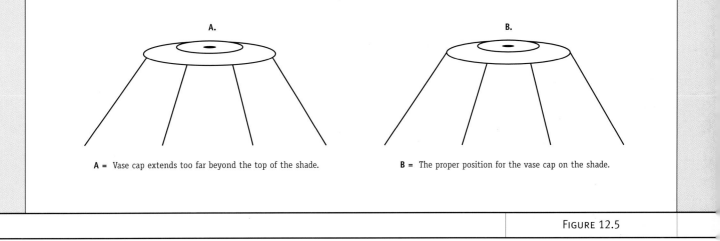

A = Vase cap extends too far beyond the top of the shade.

B = The proper position for the vase cap on the shade.

FIGURE 12.5

Select a vase cap that fits as even with the glass shade as possible. If the vase cap extends out over the glass, and beyond the points on the corners down over the glass, try the next size down. A cap that is just short of sitting directly on the points, but rests on the flat portion of the glass edge, can be used with a slight build up of solder to fill the uncovered pointed seams.

The vase cap can be attached at this time. If you want the brass vase cap to match the shade patina, you will need to add solder to the cap. Clean the cap by rubbing with 000/extra fine steel wool and hold with narrow pliers. Flux the surface and heat the cap with the solder iron at the highest setting. Add a small amount of solder (preferably 60/40 as it melts faster and stays liquid longer) and spread with the iron tip to cover the entire cap. Also, coat the inside lip under the cap with solder to help join it to the glass panels at the top. If you have trouble getting a smooth finish, hold the iron to the underside of the cap and apply the heat to melt and soothe the surface solder marks on top. If you have selected a polished cast brass decorative cap, do not tin the exterior with solder—the cap is meant to be plain. Try to add solder to the inside, underneath to "prime" prior to placing on the shade. These caps have more mass to heat than the spun metal ones, and it is easier to have some solder in place when attaching it to the inside of the shade.

6. Place the tinned vase cap on the top of the shade; sight for being level and centered on the cone. Flux and add a small amount of solder on the rim of the vase cap to flow and attach to the outside seam. Do this to all the seams on the outside.

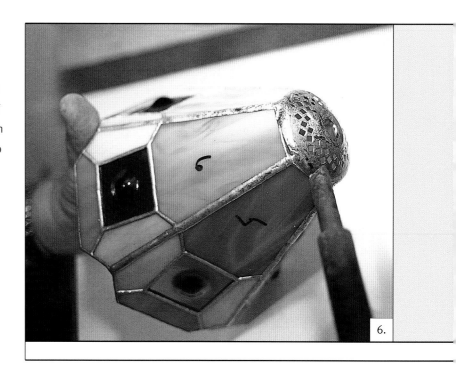

6.

Now that the vase cap is in place, the lamp is no longer flexible. Lay the shade on its side on the table and remove the masking tape from the inside. Balance the shade on a seam on the table and flux. Add small amounts of solder to attach the vase cap completely around the inside of the top of the shade. Make a raised solder line inside from the cap to the bottom edge. Always finish the inside of a shade as well as you do the outside—that is the strength of the lamp and results in a solid skeletal framework to hold the glass.

Once you have checked the seams for any bleed through or "mushrooms", wash and dry the shade. Steel wool with #ooo grade on all the seams and vase cap. This will remove any oxidation and shines the solder lines. Apply your choice of patina with a slightly damp cloth or paper towel, wash with soap and water then dry and polish the shade. Choose your lamp base and enjoy your stained glass light!

LEFT
**Pinkie**
Harold Wyman,
Bradenton, FL

6-panel scallop edge lamp made with pink/white granite opalescent (texture out) and iridescent crystal ice band.

RIGHT
**Hunter Gold**
Harold Wyman,
Bradenton, FL

6-panel straight bottom lamp made with amber/ green ripple (texture in) and sage green English Muffle stripes.

LEFT
**Moravian Star**
Pat Daley,
Kaleidoscope Stained Glass,
Sarasota, FL

Front entry light, 32" in diameter. Made with clear DeSag new antique glass and chrome-plated 1/8" copper U-channel, with a single 5" clear bulb.

ABOVE
**Dogwood Blossoms**
Tiffany-style lamp with yellow flowers built on a bell-shaped form.

ABOVE
**Rose Trellis**
John & Pat Daley,
J&P Stained Glass,
Scarborough, ME

16" round lamp with white wild roses on a red trellis, on a diamond-pieced blue sky.

LEFT
**10 Point Buck**
John & Pat Daley,
J&P Stained Glass,
Scarborough, ME

Wall sconce of deer head in brush in opalescent glass.

Courtesy of
Mr. & Mrs. Leslie Stover,
Scarborough, ME.

RIGHT
**Art Nouveau Style Lamp**
Calvin Sloan,
Star Bevel Studio,
Riverview, FL

Flared bell with ribbing.

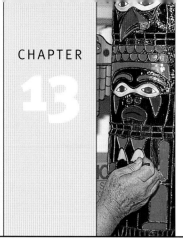

# GLass as
## SCULPTUre

The idea of this light was to commemorate the completion of a six-week road trip in Alaska that was always an ambition of Harold and Shirley Wyman. Several different techniques of working with stained glass were involved in crafting this unusual lamp to suggest the rough-hewn and hand-carved totem poles of the native Eskimo. Following is a description and photographs of the lamp in progress from drawing, to finished displayed totem.

This light is designed to be a room accent light placed on a corner table or in a wall niche in the living room near some of the photographs of Alaska taken during the trip. First, is consideration of building it to a particular height and proportion—how round should it be for stability? The decision is to build it 24" tall and the diameter of 8" across (roughly 26" flat). When designing on a curved surface such as a lamp, shape the paper pattern piece to always conform by bending it to the form. However, glass is a solid object that does not bend to follow the contour of the form, and consequently, the sides of the glass will be raised off the form, left and right of the center point on the glass. Tiffany's lamp shades work well because the small pieces fit to the shape of the lamp form—the back of the glass is almost in constant contact with the form.

Our lamp is to be built in a cylinder shape having straight vertical pieces the full height of 24" but will have to be limited in width to almost 1" in order to fit closely to the form. The two faces in the totem span almost 9" side to side, and requires bending the pieces in a kiln to follow the curvature, rather than be cut into bits spoiling them. To add further detail, the eyes, mouth and hands, fish and eagle's beak are to be painted and fired in the kiln also to avoid disrupting foil lines.

1. The appearance of a solid hewn piece of timber is not easy to convey in a light that is to be almost completely illuminated on all sides. The pattern was drawn with squares to indicate the maximum width the glass pieces can become to make the cylinder. In addition, on this totem, there are two "V" shaped grooves to create the separation of the two images and an inward taper at the top rim to seat the cap. This characteristic had to be incorporated and is accomplished by splitting and cutting a slight angle on the pieces in those three rows. The vertical strips are marked to be staggered around the light to suggest being chopped with an adze as well as to give the soldered support to the light.

2. Since there is no commercially made lamp form available in this shape or size, we make the form. Round green Styrofoam discs and thin poster board have been purchased at a local craft shop. The outline of the Styrofoam is traced onto the poster board and the circles cut out. The circles will be glued to the top and bottom of the Styrofoam. After the glue has dried, the flat discs are cut in half and glued together to form half the cylinder allowing placement on the table. By having two parts, the inside soldering can be accomplished, except for the two side seams, which will be done inside after joining. The lamp form will lie on the tabletop for

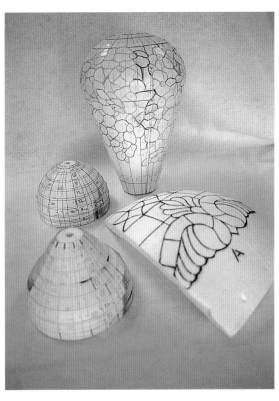

Examples of available lamp building forms.

ease of fitting the pattern and glass pieces. The two halves are now held tightly together with elastic bands so the location of the two grooves can be marked and filed into the form using a metal file. This is a joining line and must be accurately executed in order to have both completed halves solder seamlessly together.

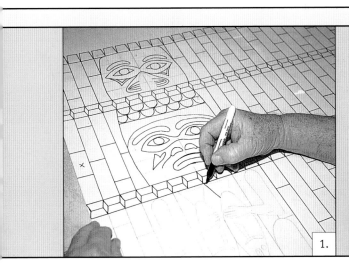

1.

2.

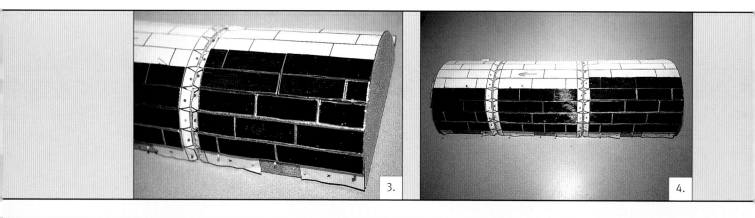

3.

4.

The pattern has been copied on a large format photocopier and cut into three segments. These are pinned to the lamp form and the glass is now chosen for the lamp. It was a difficult choice to make as using streaky gray/brown opalescent glass would be appropriate for a weather-beaten appearance, but the smoothness would have been compromised. Lighting choices are crucial, for example, a fluorescent tube bulb will hardly produce enough push to light a dense opal. It was decided the color of the wood would be a dark gold brown cathedral, easier for a fluorescent to illuminate but the texture remained an issue. The granite texture would be appealing facing out, however, the color ran vertical and the texture was horizontal, left to right. This did not result in a natural wood grain look.

3. The final choice was a thin glass with a wavy reed texture going in one direction. The pattern consists of straight cuts with various breaks. The glass is measured, cut into long strips and scored into the sizes needed. The pieces to fit in the groove will be cut and fitted into the space allotted. The back half is the simple section of the light; it is quickly foiled, soldered into place and secured with round-headed map pins.

4. The same steps are repeated on the front continuing to the areas for the figure and faces. Now in order escape cutting all the features of the totems, and have resulting solder lines marring it, the glass was chosen for its base color to closely match a photograph of a totem, upon which the design is based. On those pieces, glass enamel paint will be mixed, brushed on and fired in a tabletop kiln. The white eyes need to be two shades of blue, a dark blue iris and outlined with a pale blue background. Both mouths are solid red with a single black line in the center to indicate lips. The white hands in brown with painted fingers have to grasp blue/gray opalescent glass with painted fish. The wings on the side of the totem have painted feathers and eyespots on a blue/gray opalescent glass. The beak of the eagle is kiln formed, enamel painted and attached to a painted mouth.

The first step in enameling is to select the proper colors, which are in powdered form. The powder is mixed on a scrap of glass with a gum arabic/water based medium applied a brush full at a time until the paint flows smoothly off the brush. The painting is done on flat glass, freehand method (no marks on the glass) and as one color is applied, it is allowed to dry before adding adjoining color, for example, as on the eyes.

5.  First the center of the eyes are painted.

6.  After the irises of the eyes have dried, the second light blue on the eyes is applied.

The paint dries back to a powder form and is fired in a small kiln to 1200° Fahrenheit. When the enamel matures the colors are crisp and rich compared to the soft pastel appearance in powdered form.

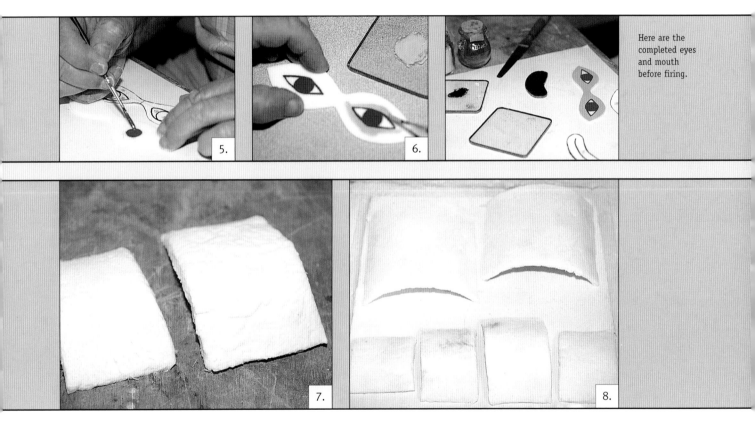

Here are the completed eyes and mouth before firing.

7.  After all the enamel painted glass is fired, molds have to be made to shape them, and the balance of the face and figure glass to be fit to the lamp form. This is accomplished by using a fiber blanket saturated with a liquid hardener added to finalize the form. The fiber blanket comes in two thicknesses: 1" or 2" in precut sizes, and the liquid hardener is available by the gallon. The forms require only 1" thickness, and three square feet of material to be purchased. The fiber blanket is cut into strips to fit the form, wetted with the hardener according to the instructions and placed over a plastic covered half of the lamp form.

8.  This is left to air dry for a few days then the semi-hard forms are lightly sanded to a smooth texture. Another coat of hardener is applied and dried.

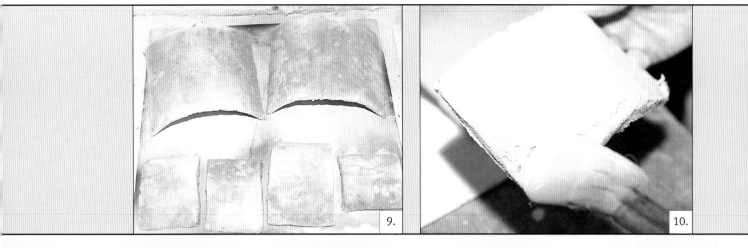

9.

10.

11.

Here are the face
and eyebrows
after slumping,
in the kiln and
still on the form.

9. A second sanding is done and then the forms can be fired in the kiln to finally dry at a higher temperature.

10. When the kiln drying is done, a powdered glass release or kiln shelf wash is mixed and brushed on the molds using a hake brush. The wash dries before two additional coats are applied and light sanded smooth with fingertips.

11. The faces are cut from the thin, wavy reed glass with the aid of a diamond band saw using an omni-directional cutting round blade. The round blade allows the glass to be cut in any direction, avoiding score lines and unwanted accidental breaks. The space for the eyebrows is initially small 1/8" pilot holes that are enlarged with a 1/4" bit to accommodate solid blue eyebrows. The blue eyebrows are dry fitted into the spaces on the forehead to ensure proper size. After the glass is cut, the pieces are assembled as close as possible without touching on the fiber blanket molds. The separate eyebrows are aligned as close to the same angle as they would appear on the face and on a separate mold to maintain the same curvature. A sample test firing of the thin reed-textured glass determined the glass slumped at 1250° Fahrenheit, and these pieces will be fired to that temperature.

12. While the large kiln is cooling down, a process that takes about 6 hours, the background reed-textured glass is cut and fitted for the area around the knees, arms and fish of the bottom figure. The arms and legs are small enough not to require slumping in the kiln but the two fish will be enameled with the eyes, mouth, gill and fins. Before this is done, the hand must be cut to pass over the fish.

13. The bodies of the fish are marked and cut to accept the hands. White glass is used for the hands, with the outlined enameled brown and black fingers painted and fired with the bodies of the fish in the tabletop kiln.

14. As the table kiln cools, about an hour and a half, the bottom face is assembled and soldered in position. After the hands and fish cool, they will also be foiled and soldered in place.

The two halves to the totem light are ready for joining by moving down the two side seams, following the soldering of the other faces on the lamp form. Soldering the outside seam first is easiest with the inside going slower due to limited space. The pedestal for the base is made of oak and is 12" square with a $1^1/_2$" high round piece to fit up inside the bottom of the cylinder.

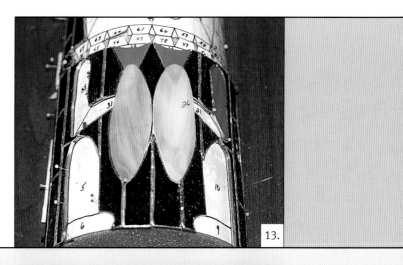

13.

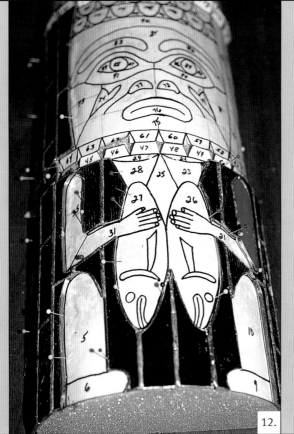

12.

14.

This has been drilled to accept the lamp wire cord as well as a threaded rod with which to attach the electrical works. The idea is to avoid "hot spots". In addition, two light bulbs would show through the cathedral amber brown glass. A continuous light source is required to illuminate the cylinder and the only solution is a fluorescent light fixture being stood on end and centered as much as possible in the space.

15. An 18" fluorescent light was selected. Using brass pipe elbow fittings and threaded hollow rod, the light was attached to the brass support. The top of the pipe work extends up through a handmade cap and secures the lamp with a finial at the base.

16. The vase cap is required to finish the open top of the lamp. It's a subtle shape to mesh with the balance of the lamp, and to have two glass "ears"

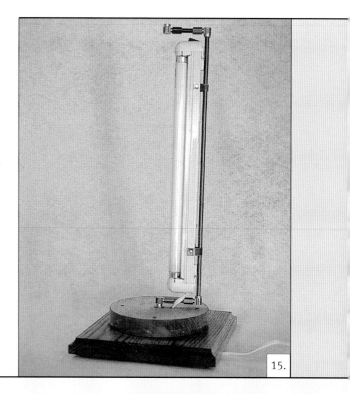

15.

16.

17.

attached at the top. Sheet copper is cut in a 9" circle with kerf cuts made $1^1/_8$" in, for folding and to fit inside the top of the lamp. The copper is hammered to roundness on the rim of the folds with planishing hammers on a lead slab. The cap requires careful fitting into the opening prior to soldering in place. After the cap is shaped, it is tinned with 60/40 solder and drilled in the center to accommodate the pass-through of the finial screw. Four holes are drilled to relieve any heat

build up from the light fixture and the cap is soldered to the top of the lamp. The glass "ears" are attached to the cap and the two wings are secured to the side seams.

17. The solder is lightly rubbed with #ooo steel wool and cleaned before applying black patina. The fingers on the fired hands need slight touch up with "cold paint", namely black oil base enamel. Once this is achieved and the glass polished with a finishing wax, the totem is complete.

**Alaskan Totem Light**
Harold Wyman,
Bradenton, FL

Freestanding light of
a totem pole using kiln-
shaped and fired enamel
glass, assembled on a
handmade form.

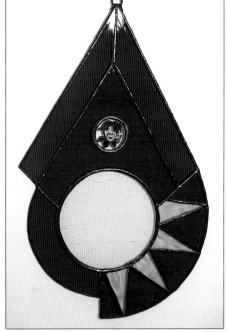

RIGHT
**Woodland Fairy**
Pat Daley,
Kaleidoscope Stained Glass,
Sarasota, FL

Painted and fired glass
based on a design from
"Fairies", by Jillian Sawyer.

ABOVE
**The Jester**
Pat Daley & Harold Wyman,
Bradenton, FL

Copper foil abstract with
enameled face of a jester
in smaller rondel.

# STAINED GLASS:
## BEYOND THE WINDOW

By this point I trust you are convinced glass is an extremely versatile medium. The creation of a glass item using bevels, dichroic, flashed glass or just a simple panel begins with an idea. Colored drawings help to visualize the desired result. The line drawing for a beveled heron can only indicate the shape of the clear bevels and therefore, a guide for the pattern. The flow of the leaded lines can guide your eyes smoothly into the center as in the beveled crystal cross, or you can note the uneven, jagged black and white frame surrounding a Chinese word. The simple Celtic pattern etched in red on green flashed glass eliminates all cut lines, but makes a strong statement regarding the design flow.

**Butterfly and Vine**
Pat Daley,
Kaleidoscope Stained
Glass,
Sarasota, FL

Copper foil pattern panel.

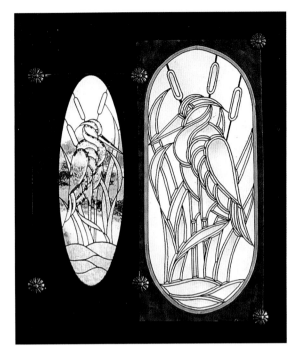

LEFT
**Beveled Heron**
Calvin Sloan,
Star Bevel Studio,
Riverview, FL

Shown along side the
working drawing.

RIGHT
**Celtic Pattern**
Pat Daley,
Kaleidoscope
Stained Glass,
Sarasota, FL

An example of flash glass
—red on green antique.

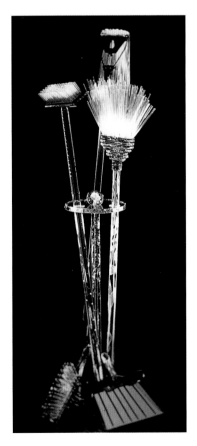

ABOVE
**Chinese Chop**
Tammy Kahler,
Sarasota, FL

LEFT
**Clean Sweep**
Calvin Sloan,
Star Bevel Studio,
Riverview, FL

Life-size glass rod, plate
and mirror sculpture of a
broom, mop, brushes and
dust tray.

BELOW
**Da Dao**
Teri Bernard-Sokoloff

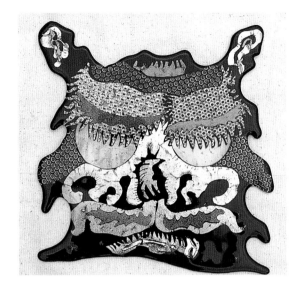

BELOW
**Da Dao**
Teri Bernard-Sokoloff

Stained glass has been used to illustrate nature and people for centuries as seen in the butterfly panel and two stylized portraits. Dichroic glass and fusing have paired together to expand the glass artist's horizons to give shape to their inner vision. The fusing process is becoming mainstream with glass crafters as the technique is cut, placed and fused to build panels with fewer or no lead or solder lines, creating special effects with the glass.

ABOVE
**My Aunt**
Garth Edwards

RIGHT
**Futility of War**
Richard Setti,
Sarasota, FL

Made in 1974-75. Use of glass as a medium for expressing social issues. This piece is on display at Glass Crafters in Sarasota, FL.

Glass can be mixed with other media and fashioned into something new. For example, the Iron Butterfly has foiled glass soldered into the cut openings in the wings, while the broken, antique Pierpoint painted shade was reconstructed to become a electrified wall sconce. The soft-focus reverse painting will glow again with new glass added to fit the wall mounting. A black wrought iron (lantern) framework, forgotten in a cellar, has been cleaned and painted. Panels using antique pressed jewels and seedy mouth blown glass have been inserted, and with the addition of a candelabra cluster is now enjoyed as a light in the master bathroom.

LEFT AND BELOW
**Iron Butterfly**
Paul Barsalou,
Bradenton, FL

ABOVE
**Wrought Iron Lantern**
Pat Daley,
Kaleidoscope Stained Glass,
Sarasota, FL

ABOVE
**Pierpoint Shade/Suncatcher**
Pat Daley,
Kaleidoscope Stained Glass,
Sarasota, FL

LEFT
**Bevel Gazebo**
Pat Daley,
Kaleidoscope Stained Glass,
Sarasota, FL

Table planter made with
bevels and frosted glass.
Twisted wire and a clear
marble finial with pewter
patina highlight this
five-sided item.

BELOW
**Glass Houses**
Wilbur Seymour,
Riverview, FL

ABOVE
**Casket Incense Box**
Pat Daley,
Kaleidoscope Stained Glass,
Sarasota, FL

White iridescent box with
a copper wirework lid and
nugget jewel for burning
stick incense.

RIGHT
**Rosebud Sconce**
Pat Daley,
Kaleidoscope Stained Glass,
Sarasota, FL

Small votive candle
wall sconce in the Art
Nouveau style.

Stained glass is also worked into functional,
practical items—no matter how mundane they
may seem. The glass votive candleholder is
enriched with a color setting or the simple aromas
of incense are dispersed from a decorative glass
box-type burner. Table planters, mirrors, clocks,
Kleenex box covers, an abundance of useful or decorative dimensional items can be fashioned using
glass. Pattern books are available for many of
these items as well as relying on your imagination.

RIGHT
**The Chosen**
Marie Sovell,
Oak Park, MI

Use of grey white
streaky opal glass makes
an interesting effect as
a charcoal portrait in
this leaded panel.

BELOW
**Strap-On Features**
Garth Edwards

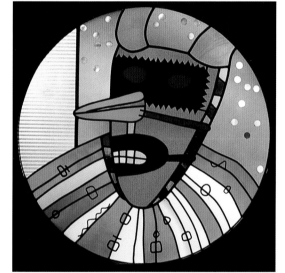

BELOW
**Year of Roses**
Harold & Shirley
Wyman,
Bradenton, FL

The installation
of "Year of Roses"
transom window is
shown at the left.

The foundation of all stained glass creations
is still the design, cut, fit and assembly using
proper methods for the project, and on occa-
sion, teamwork is necessary on installations.
However, when completed, the end result of
all the work is to be appreciated and enjoyed
over a lifetime.

## KEEPSAKE BOX PATTERN

Overall pattern to fit on 6 x 12" piece of glass.

BOX LID

Measures 6 x 5$^7/_8$"

6" wide overall before cutting.

1/4" WASTE

1¼"   BOX FRONT   1¼"

1¼"   LEFT SIDE   1⅝"

WASTE

1¼"   RIGHT SIDE   1⅝"

1⅝"   BOX BACK   1⅝"

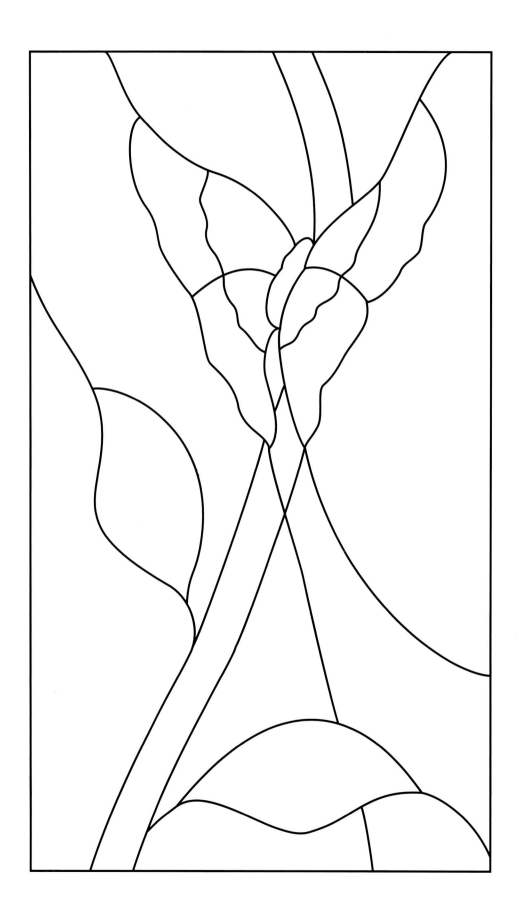

**abrasion:** the process of grinding away the top surface of a piece of flashed glass. A diamond coated burr or grinding wheel may be used to accomplish this.

**antique glass:** sheet glass made by the centuries old method of mouth blowing. The glass is blown into cylinders. The closed end of the cylinder is cut off and the side cut to flatten into a sheet.

**breaking the score:** separating a piece of glass into planned sections along a marked and scored line.

**cartoon/drawing:** the line drawing for a work of glass with all cut lines shown. Individual pieces may be numbered and color shadings indicated. A second copy is cut for pattern pieces.

**cathedral glass:** transparent, colored glass, machine made to uniform 1/8" thickness and either smooth or with a choice of textures.

**composition:** the overall design of a finished piece with proper color balance and line design.

**copper foiled glass:** glass that is wrapped with adhesive-backed copper strips and completely soldered front and back to create a flat or dimensional object.

**cut line:** the thin line drawn on glass to score with the glasscutter.

**dalle de verre:** a thick slab of stained glass (8"x 11"x 1") for use with epoxy or cement. Can be chipped and faceted for a jewel-like effect using the copper foil technique.

**etching:** method of removing one layer of color from flashed glass in a hydrofluoric acid bath. The glass to be etched is exposed via cutting a stencil from a completely covered piece of glass. Available softer etching creams "cloud" the exposed surface on cathedral glass but will not work on flashed glass. *(Hydrofluoric acid attacks and dissolves glass and is very dangerous to handle.)*

**flashed glass:** one sheet of glass made of two layers of color. Any color can be flashed on top of another, for example: blue on clear, red on yellow, red on green, etc. This glass enjoys heavy use for etching to avoid cutting distracting lines in a design, or for the particular shade or variations of color produced when using mouth blown flashed glass.

**fusing:** the technique of controlled melting of combinations of glass in layers using a kiln. This requires knowledge of the individual pieces of glass as to the coefficient of expansion (C.O.E.) rate so that compatible glass is used to avoid different heating and cooling movement. Glass that does not have the same C.O.E. rate will shatter in the kiln or within hours during cooling due to internal stress. Required high temperatures can range from 1550° to 1750°.

**enamels:** soft powdered colored glass that is mixed with a medium and painted onto the glass with a brush. When the medium is dry, the glass is placed in a kiln for firing to temperatures ranging from 1250° to 1350°.

**glass bending:** the shaping of glass over (draping) or into (sagging) a mold by placing the flat glass onto the mold and firing in a kiln. The temperature required for bending glass are not as high as fusing, usually around 1350° to 1400°.

**glass globs or nuggets:** thick, rounded pieces of glass, usually cathedral colors available in plain or iridescent. Size ranges from 1/2" to 1" and are free-form rounded shapes.

**glass jewels:** these cathedral or opalescent glass have been pressed into steel molds and then polished for consistent shapes and sizes. Facetted round, navettes and square shapes; smooth ovals and rounds, raised swirls and "iceberg" shapes are just a few of the types of jewels available.

**glass thickness:** this can vary from 3/16" of an inch on the thinnest edge of mouthblown antique, up to almost 1/2" on the opposite side of the same sheet. The sheet of antique glass may not be completely flat for cutting and should have a towel or soft cushion material placed under it for cutting. Machine made glass is consistently 1/8" but can have a soft pebble or a high, rough ripple or folded drape-textured effect to increase thickness.

**granite-back glass:** a type of texture with one smooth side and the opposite slightly rough.

**grozzing:** snipping away the excess small points of glass, along the scored edge of glass, that did not break away cleanly. Use the curved, small fine tooth portion of the breaker/grozers to wear the glass down.

**hammered glass:** usually this texture is applied to cathedral glass but can also be found on opalescent. It takes the shape of small round marks resembling indents in metal made with a ball peen hammer. These can be consistently placed in rows in round, slightly elongated and irregular shapes depending on the glass manufacturer.

**hydrofluoric acid:** the only liquid material that will dissolve silica—the main ingredient in glass. The length of exposure to this corrosive acid will determine how far the acid will eat into the glass.
*It is extremely hazardous material and all safety precautions are mandatory to protect your skin and the air you inhale.*

**joint:** in the lead came technique, the point where lead lines meet one another. The joints usually butt one against the other.

**kiln:** a chamber made of firebrick in which to bend or fuse glass. Size ranges from small tabletop units to 3' x 4' bed, floor models. They can be electric or gas heated, use pyrometers to measure temperature and have shut-off controls tripped by ceramic "cones" or computerized timers.

**knapping:** the process of faceting slab "dalle" glass by chipping at the edges to flake off rainbow-shaped pieces with the slab glass hammer.

**lead came:** extruded pure lead that is milled to specific dimensions as either "U" or "H" shaped strips, then cut and formed to accept and hold the stained glass shape. It's available in spools or precut lengths of about 6 feet.

**leaded glass:** glass held together by lead cames, soldered at all abutting joints.

**leading:** assembling a work of stained glass where lead came is holding the material together.

**mold:** high temperature fired shapes into which glass can be draped over, or sagged into. These can be commercially made terra cotta or stainless steel forms. Free-shaped forms can be created with resin impregnated refractory fabric, or hand carved from soft firebrick.

**mold release:** a dry powder mixed with water to a thin consistency that is brushed onto the surface of the mold to prevent the glass from sticking at a high temperature. It is also used on kiln shelves.

**opalescent glass:** non-transparent glass where the colors are presented by reflected light.

**oxidation:** the dull, tough, outer covering on lead came that occurs with exposure to air and must be removed with a wire brush prior to soldering. It's the dull finish on copper foil that was not soldered promptly. This can be removed by light rubbing with #000 or extra fine steel wool.

**pattern:** the paper template which is placed on the glass surface for tracing prior to cutting.

**pontil:** the blowpipe used in gathering and blowing molten glass.

**pot glass:** glass that is of one solid color, no texture and extremely opaque with no light transmitted. Two examples are solid, dense white and black.

**pot metal:** the medieval name for the molten glass batch. It was heated in a large crucible and metallic oxides were added for color.

**reamies:** sheets of antique glass with faint, delicate streaks of color swept through it.

**reinforcing bars:** galvanized steel rods used to span a lead or copper foil window to prevent it from bowing.

**resist material:** used to protect areas of glass during acid etching or sandblasting procedures.

**rolled edges:** The smooth but uneven wavy sides of raw sheet glass from the lehr. This must be cut away to gain a straight side. Few manufacturers leave these edges untrimmed, while others, producing larger sheets, cut them for recycling.

**sandblasting:** another method of removing glass from a specific area where a design within the panel.

**seedy glass:** cathedral glass that has small elongated air bubbles trapped inside.

**score:** the line imposed by a glass cutting wheel upon the surface of the glass. This "fracture line" weakens the surface tension of the glass and allows it to be broken in a controlled manner.

**semi-antique glass or new antique:** machine made glass with little surface marking or texture but with brilliant, jewel-like tones.

**solder bead:** the solder build up on copper foil, to a rounded shape, for strength and appearance.

**spot tack:** the melting of a small amount of solder onto the copper foiled pieces of glass at joints, or the center of a line in order to secure the pieces, preventing movement.

**streakies:** glass sheets with streaks of color running through them. Colors may be varied against a background of yet another color, either in opalescent or cathedral glass.

**tapping:** one of the methods of breaking a score. A ball-ended glasscutter is used to tap along the score from underneath to shock the score into breaking. A change in "glass resonance" while tapping will indicate the score has started to break.

**tinning:** the application of a thin coat of solder completely covering the surface of another metal to stiffen it. This is usually performed when you are unable to continue the complete soldering of the work, after spot tacking the glass pieces together. By doing this, you avoid oxidation on the copper foil.

# index